REBE

Greene, Alexis.
Rebeck in an hour

ur

BY ALEXIS GREENE

SUSAN C. MOORE, SERIES EDITOR

PLAYWRIGHTS in an hour
know the playwright, love the play

IN AN HOUR BOOKS • HANOVER, NEW HAMPSHIRE • INANHOURBOOKS.COM
AN IMPRINT OF SMITH AND KRAUS PUBLISHERS, INC • SMITHANDKRAUS.COM

With grateful thanks to Carl R. Mueller, whose
fascinating introductions to his translations of
the Greek and German playwrights provided
inspiration for this series.

Published by In an Hour Books
an imprint of Smith and Kraus, Inc.
177 Lyme Road, Hanover, NH 03755
inanhourbooks.com SmithandKraus.com

Know the playwright, love the play.

In an Hour, In a Minute, and Theater IQ are registered trademarks of
In an Hour Books.

ABSTRACT EXPRESSION. © 1998 by Madwoman in the Attic, Inc. Reprinted by permission of the author.
For performance rights, contact Samuel French, Inc., 45 W. 25th St., New York, NY 10010.
(www.samuelfrench.com) (212-206-8990)

THE ACTRESS. © 2002 by Madwoman in the Attic, Inc. Reprinted by permission of the author.
For performance rights, contact George Lane, Creative Artists Agncy (glane@caa.com).

BAD DATES. © 2004 by Madwoman in the Attic, Inc. Reprinted by permission of the author.
For performance rights, contact Samuel French, Inc., 45 W. 25th St., New York, NY 10010.
(www.samuelfrench.com) (212-206-8990)

THE BELLS. © 2005 by Madwoman in the Attic, Inc. Reprinted by permission of the author. For
performance rights, contact George Lane, Creative Artists Agncy (glane@caa.com).

THE SCENE. © 2006 by Madwoman in the Attic, Inc. Reprinted by permission of the author.
For performance rights, contact Samuel French, Inc., 45 W. 25th St., New York, NY 10010.
(www.samuelfrench.com) (212-206-8990)

Front cover design by Dan Mehling, dmehling@gmail.com
Text design by Kate Mueller, Electric Dragon Productions
Book production by Dede Cummings Design, DCDesign@sover.net

ISBN-13: 978-1-936232-22-2
ISBN-10: 1-936232-22-7
Library of Congress Control Number: 2009943231

CONTENTS

Why Playwrights in an Hour?

This new series by Smith and Kraus Publishers titled Playwrights in an Hour has a dual purpose for being: one academic, the other general. For the general reader, this volume, as well as the many others in the series, offers in compact form the information needed for a basic understanding and appreciation of the works of each volume's featured playwright. Which is not to say that there don't exist volumes on end devoted to each playwright under consideration. But inasmuch as few are blessed with enough time to read the splendid scholarship that is available, a brief, highly focused accounting of the playwright's life and work is in order. The central feature of the series, a thirty- to forty-page essay, integrates the playwright into the context of his or her time and place. The volumes, though written to high standards of academic integrity, are accessible in style and approach to the general reader as well as to the student and, of course, to the theater professional and theatergoer. These books will serve for the brushing up of one's knowledge of a playwright's career, to the benefit of theater work or theatergoing. The Playwrights in an Hour series represents all periods of Western theater: Aeschylus to Shakespeare to Wedekind to Ibsen to Williams to Beckett, and on to the great contemporary playwrights who continue to offer joy and enlightenment to a grateful world.

Carl R. Mueller
School of Theater, Film, and Television
Department of Theater
University of California, Los Angeles

Introduction

Sigmund Freud once got himself in a lot of hot water by asking "What do women want?" An equally inflammatory question today might be, "What do women playwrights want?" The obvious answer is that women playwrights want the same things as their male counterparts — access to production, percentage of the gross, audience admiration, critical endorsements, coveted prizes, and inscriptions on the walls of fame. After so many years of pressing their faces against the sweetshop window, they desire and deserve the chocolates and caramels on display.

Theresa Rebeck has been working hard and productively over recent years to get a place at the candy counter. Judging by her prodigious creative output, she is a continuously evolving artist. Judging by the quality of her plays, she is a truly independent spirit. The best of Rebeck's theatrical writing, like that of all good writers, has always been gender neutral. From Lillian Hellman (who made Regina Hubbard in *The Little Foxes* even more ruthless than her male counterparts) to Paula Vogel (who short-circuited the prevailing assumptions about child abuse in *How I Learned to Drive* and about pornography in *Hot 'n' Throbbing*) to Suzan-Lori Parks (who resented being told "my plays are about what it's about to be black — as if that's all we think about. My life is not about race. It's about being alive") to Wendy Wasserstein (who satirized gender studies and political correctness in *Third*), not to mention dozens of other gifted woman writers — the best of them, whether embracing feminist politics or not, have usually managed to avoid ideological clichés.

Rebeck is as sophisticated about these issues as any woman writing. She has not only composed many plays, she has mastered many forms, including television and the novel. The play she collaborated on with Alexandra Gersten-Vassilaros, called *Omnium Gatherum*, holds a high place as the *locus classicus* of dramatic works about 9/11, featuring one of the most goofy radical-chic dinner parties since Shaw's *Heartbreak House*. Her recent play *Mauritius* is less about politics than about stamp collecting. *Spike Heels* is a poisonously funny sex triangle featuring hilariously abusive dialogue.

Although a declared feminist, Rebeck almost never falls into stereotypes as a writer, though she has been quoted, in the introduction to her *Collected Plays Volume I, 1989–1998,* as saying that "gender bias is the hidden sin of the American theatre." More importantly, though, is the fact that Rebeck's playwriting is almost entirely free of such reductionism. Her true subject, as she correctly says, is not gender issues but what it means to be an American, "the way David Hare examines what it means to be British or Brian Friel examines what it means to be Irish." Rebeck knows that she cannot ignore the social issues of the day, but she recognizes, like Chekhov, that it is not her job to solve problems, only to present them correctly.

This is something she has done with genuine gusto in her adaptation of Aeschylus' *Agamemnon, The Water's Edge,* and even better in her electrifying comedy *The Scene.* In the latter play, Rebeck demonstrates how effectively she can transcend discursive chatter, and get on with writing a lively account of the aesthetic and moral failures of show folk. Actually, the play is not unlike David Rabe's *Hurlyburly,* a similar probe into entertainment culture, with the same raucous and remorseless exposure of human folly.

I have full confidence that Rebeck will continue to pour her creative imagination into artistry in the coming years. She has enough smarts, enough energy, and enough fearlessness to stand among her most gifted contemporaries — and thus be assured a permanent place in the sweetshop of American dramatic literature.

Robert Brustein
Founding Director of the Yale and American Repertory Theatres
Distinguished Scholar in Residence, Suffolk University
Senior Research Fellow, Harvard University

Rebeck

IN A MINUTE

AGE	DATE	
—	**1960**	**Enter Theresa Rebeck.**
1	1961	The Orient Express, from Paris to Bucharest, takes its last ride.
2	1962	Edward Albee — *Who's Afraid of Virginia Woolf*
3	1963	Betty Freidan — *The Feminine Mystique*
7	1967	Charles de Gaulle declares "Long live free Quebec!" in Montreal.
9	1969	Lorraine Hansberry — *A Raisin in the Sun*
11	1971	Postal strike in Britain means no mail for forty-seven days.
14	1974	Defying church law, four U.S. Episcopal bishops ordain eleven women as priests.
15	1975	With capture of Saigon, Vietnam War ends.
16	1976	Alan Ayckbourn — *The Norman Conquests*
21	1981	Sandra Day O'Connor is the first woman on the Supreme Court.
25	1985	UK starts to screen blood donations for AIDS.
27	1987	Paul Simon's "Graceland" is a hit.
28	**1988**	**Theresa Rebeck — *Sunday on the Rocks***
31	1991	Only 12 percent of West Germans approve of a unified Germany.
32	1992	Disney opens its "Euro Disney" theme park in Paris.
33	**1993**	**Theresa Rebeck — *Loose Knit***
34	**1994**	**Theresa Rebeck — *The Family of Mann***
35	1995	Timothy McVeigh's Oklahoma City bombing kills 168.
36	1996	Harold Pinter — *Ashes to Ashes*
37	1997	Woolworth's shutters its discount stores nationwide.
39	1999	In Chicago, Michael Jordan announces that he will retire.
40	**2000**	**Theresa Rebeck — *The Butterfly Collection***
41	2001	The Taliban destroys the ancient Buddhas of Bamiyan in Afghanistan.
42	2002	*A Beautiful Mind* wins Oscar for the best picture.
43	**2003**	**Theresa Rebeck — *Bad Dates***
44	2004	N.J. Governor James McGreevey announces on television that he's gay and resigns.
45	**2005**	**Theresa Rebeck — *The Bells***
46	2006	Pope Benedict XVI issues his first encyclical, "God Is Love."
49	**2009**	**Theresa Rebeck — *The Understudy***

A snapshot of the playwright's world. From historical events to pop-culture and the literary landscape of the time, this brief list catalogues events that directly or indirectly impacted the playwright's writing. Play citations refer to premiere dates.

FULL-LENGTH PLAYS

Sunday on the Rocks

Spike Heels

Loose Knit

The Family of Mann

Rhinoceros (adaptation of play by Eugene Ionesco)

A View of the Dome

Abstract Expression

The Butterfly Collection

Dollhouse

Bad Dates

Omnium Gatherum (with Alexandra Gersten-Vassilaros)

The Bells

The Scene

The Water's Edge

Mauritius

Our House

The Understudy

The Novelist

ONE-ACT PLAYS

Does This Woman Have a Name?

Sex with the Censor

Big Mistake

Drinking Problem

Candy Heart

What We're Up Against

This section presents a complete list of the playwright's works in chronological order.

Katie and Frank
The Contract
Great to See You
Walk
The First Day
Josephina
Funeral Play
Art Appreciation
The Actress
Deliver Me
Train to Brooklyn
How We Get to Where We're Going
Off Base
Aftermath
Mary, Mother of God, Intercede for Us

MUSICALS
The Two Orphans

TELEVISION
American Dreamer
Dream On
Brooklyn Bridge
LA Law
NYPD Blue
Total Security
Maximum Bob
Third Watch
Law & Order: Criminal Intent
South
Canterbury's Law

FILMS
Harriet the Spy
Gossip

Onstage with Rebeck

Introducing Colleagues and Contemporaries
of Theresa Rebeck

 THEATER

Beth Henley, American playwright

Emily Mann, American playwright, director, and artistic director, McCarter Theater Center

Lynne Meadow, American founder and artistic director, Manhattan Theatre Club

Julia Miles, American founder, The Women's Project

James Nicola, American artistic director, New York Theatre Workshop

Paula Vogel, American playwright

Wendy Wasserstein, American playwright

Julie White, American actress

 ARTS

George Balanchine, Russian-born choreographer and director, New York City Ballet

Willem de Kooning, American Abstract Expressionist painter

Bob Dylan, American singer and songwriter

Tina Fey, American TV comedian and actress

Nora Jones, American singer and musician

John Lennon, English singer and songwriter (The Beatles)

Dmitri Shostakovitch, Russian composer

Twyla Tharp, American choreographer

 FILM

Kathryn Bigelow, American director

Catherine Breillat, French filmmaker and novelist

This section lists contemporaries whom the playwright may or may not have known.

Francis Ford Coppola, American director
Spike Lee, American director
George Lucas, American director
Robert Redford, American actor and director
Martin Scorsese, American director
Kevin Smith, American director

POLITICS/MILITARY

Bella Abzug, American politician
George H. W. Bush, president of the United States
George W. Bush, president of the United States
Hillary Clinton, New York state senator and secretary of state
    under Barack Obama
Lyndon Baines Johnson, president of the United States
Richard M. Nixon, president of the United States
Alice Paul, American author of the Equal Rights Amendment
Ronald Reagan, president of the United States

SCIENCE

Hans Bethe, German-American physicist
Linda Buck, American biologist
Gertrude B. Elion, American biochemist
Jane Goodall, English primatologist
Stephen Hawking, English physicist
Rita Levi-Montalcini, Italian neurologist
Barbara McClintock, American Nobel Laureate cytogeneticist
Rosalind Yalow, American physicist

LITERATURE

Margaret Atwood, Canadian novelist and poet
John Barth, American novelist
Donald Barthelme, American novelist
Simone de Beauvoir, French theorist
Louise Erdrich, American novelist
Toni Morrison, American novelist

Alice Munro, Canadian short-story writer
Adrienne Rich, American poet

RELIGION/PHILOSOPHY

Karl Barth, Swiss Reformed theologian
Daniel Dennett, American philosopher
Sister Barbara Ferraro, pro-choice Roman Catholic nun
Sister Patricia Hussey, pro-choice Roman Catholic nun
Pope John Paul II
Martin Luther King Jr., American minister and civil rights leader
John Rawls, American philosopher
Elie Wiesel, Jewish theologian

SPORTS

Bonnie Blair, American speed skater
Brandi Chastain, American soccer player
Nadia Comaneci, Russian gymnast and Olympic gold medalist
Dale Earnhardt Jr., American race car driver
Chris Evert, American tennis champion
Birgit Fischer, East German–born kayaker and Olympic gold
     medalist
Donna de Varona, American Olympic swimmer
Joan Samuelson, American marathon runner

INDUSTRY/BUSINESS

Michael R. Bloomberg, American founder, Bloomberg L.P.,
     a financial software company
Bill Gates, American founder, Microsoft
Lynn Elsenhans, American president and CEO, Sunoco
Steve Jobs, American cofounder and CEO, Apple, Inc.
Ellen Kullman, American CEO, DuPont
Michael Milken, American investor
Jack Welch, American former CEO, General Electric
Andrea Wong, American president and CEO, Lifetime Networks

REBECK

in an
hour

A CATHOLIC GIRLHOOD

Theresa Rebeck was born in Cincinnati, Ohio. Her father, George Rebeck, worked as a metallurgical engineer, while her mother, Joan Rebeck, raised Rebeck and her five brothers and sisters and often volunteered as a social worker. Brought up as a Catholic, Rebeck was exposed to what she calls a "patriarchal religion," which she found difficult to handle and believes has informed her plays. The message she received was "You're a girl, and you're supposed to do what you're told." However, Rebeck went to a progressive, all-girls Catholic high school, Ursuline Academy, which she found liberating when it came to attitudes about spirituality and social justice.

Young Rebeck developed a love of the arts. She took piano lessons and went to the theater. The first play she saw was a production of Molière's *Tartuffe* at Cincinnati Playhouse in the Park, and she remembers it as "a riveting experience." Indeed, at the age of sixteen, she announced to her mother that she wanted to be a playwright, a decision that was met with horror and bewilderment. This was a supportive but

This is the core of the book. The essay places the playwright in the context of his or her world and analyzes the influences and inspirations within that world.

traditional family, and the Rebecks expected their children to do practical things with their lives.

Still, from the beginning Rebeck was a rebel. "The role that I played within my family was the problem child, because I talked back. I got used to being the voice of contention," she recalled, "but it was a difficult position."

It was a position she would carry into her dramatic writing and her career.

PLAYWRIGHT OR PROFESSOR?

After graduating from Ursuline Academy in 1976, Rebeck went to college at the University of Notre Dame in Indiana, and then traveled East to Brandeis University for graduate school because "they liked women there and they had no football team." After Notre Dame, those were big plusses. Brandeis also offered a commitment to humanistic ideals, a reverence for learning, and a deep commitment to the arts, all of which enticed Rebeck. The school's motto is "Truth even unto its innermost parts," which she thought "a beautiful and mysterious ideal." At Brandeis, she received three degrees: an M.A. in English in 1983, an M.F.A. in dramatic writing in 1986, and in 1989 a Ph.D. in Victorian literature. For her dissertation, she analyzed the melodramas *The Bells, Les Deux Orphelines (The Two Orphans), Masks and Faces,* and *The Poor of London.* (She would later write her own version of *The Bells* and co-author a musical based on *Les Deux Orphelines.*)

As Rebeck describes her graduate education, she followed the playwriting and Ph.D. tracks almost simultaneously. Doubting her worth as a writer, even though in her heart that is what she wished to be, she committed herself to finishing the doctorate in case she needed a teaching job to support herself.

"Then I realized that it was a matter of giving myself permission to embrace playwriting, that it wasn't something I had to earn by virtue of being good enough or smart enough (I think I got that from the church). So I embraced it . . ."

She has no regrets about completing the Ph.D., however. The study provided a window onto a period in British history when theater was a glorious and powerful force in the culture, in stark contrast, Rebeck feels, to how theater is regarded now, especially in the United States. Everybody went to the theater in the nineteenth century, Rebeck observes, from aristocrats to shopgirls. She believes that, by comparison, contemporary theater and its audiences tend to be elitist.

Studying Victorian melodrama also influenced Rebeck's playwriting, even though most of Rebeck's characters are, on the surface at least, more liberated emotionally and sexually than their Victorian forbears. Melodrama has influenced Rebeck's disciplined sense of structure, her yen for theatrical surprise, and even her plots. She herself points to *Spike Heels*, written soon after finishing her dissertation and produced as a workshop in July 1990 by New York Stage and Film Company in association with Vassar College's Powerhouse Theater. In the dissertation, Rebeck had discussed hero-heroine-villain triangles. *Spike Heels* involves a sensual, somewhat rough-around-the-edges secretary named Georgie, who is sought after by the play's supposed hero, Andrew, and by Georgie's crude, aggressive, sexually demonstrative boss, Edward — presumably the villain of the piece.

"In melodrama," Rebeck explained, "the villain and the hero both want the body of the heroine. The villain wants to rape her, the hero wants to marry her. There's this whole social tension resting on that woman's body." She began writing *Spike Heels* and realized that Andrew was playing the role of the traditional hero. He wants to tame Georgie and domesticate her, while Edward wants to take her to bed. But is Andrew truly the good guy and Edward truly dastardly? Rebeck flipped the stereotypes and played with the hero-heroine-villain triangle. Andrew, trapped within a set of rules, tries to control Georgie and force her into his image of the proper woman. Edward relishes Georgie the way she is. At the end, Georgie rejects the Pygmalion figure that has "created" her and selects the pleasure-loving, life-embracing Edward, who may prove a cad but at least is honest about his desires.

Spike Heels opened Off Broadway at Second Stage Theatre in June 1992, starring Kevin Bacon, Tony Goldwyn, and Julie White. The issue of sexual harassment that the play addressed was timely, for Americans had recently spent hours in front of their televisions, enthralled by the testimony of law professor Anita Hill, who claimed she had been sexually harassed by Supreme Court nominee Clarence Thomas. Perhaps because of that theme, which is as relevant today as it was in 1992 — and also because of the lively interplay among the four characters — *Spike Heels* is produced regularly across the country and is a particular favorite with college students.

THE THERESA REBECK STYLE

Having chosen playwriting over teaching, Rebeck began the challenging process of learning to write a good play. She looks back on graduate school as a period when fantasies about the sort of dramatist she wished to be gave way to discovering the reality of her particular style. "When you're in graduate school and young, you say, 'I'm going to be [Samuel] Beckett. This is what the shape of an artist is.' I was trying to write stuff that I had no way of knowing how to do."

An early one-act that later became the full-length *Sunday on the Rocks* revealed to Rebeck that she wrote best when writing the world as she saw it. The opening scene of *Sunday* has three women — three roommates — sitting on a porch one Sunday morning, drinking scotch for breakfast and talking about men, relationships, life. The dialogue sounds unselfconscious, specific to each character, and truthful. "We all have a particular keyhole through which we see the world," Rebeck once said, "and our job as writers is to keep the keyhole clean and report what we see. I see sexism more strongly than other people do. I learned from *Sunday on the Rocks* that you start with how you see the world and build on that."

From *Sunday on the Rocks* and *Spike Heels*, Rebeck also learned that she could be funny. She thought *Spike Heels* was a dark, angry play until, at a reading, the audience roared with laughter. Rebeck attributes her comic ability to growing up in a large family, where comedy was a survival tactic and she competed to be the funniest person in the room. Whatever the source of her comedic skill, her earliest plays demonstrate wit and an inclination to satirize what she sees on the other side of that keyhole. During the first decade of her career, approximately 1988 to 1998, Rebeck's acute ear for how contemporary urban men and women talk, and her determination to dramatize them as fallible combinations of the best and the worst, moved her plays into the realm of comedies of manners.

THE PLAYWRIGHT IS A WOMAN

Early in her playwriting career, Rebeck came up against a dilemma with which she continues to wrestle: the American theater's tendency to dismiss female dramatists as not being up to the standard of male dramatists.

She often recounts a conversation that took place at a Boston dinner party shortly after *Sunday on the Rocks* received its premiere at the New Ehrlich Theater Company in 1988. A male director turned to her and said, "Maybe you can tell me. Why can't women ever transcend their identities as women and just write as playwrights?" Rebeck responded, "Do you mean, why can't we write like men?" The director said no, that wasn't what he meant. But according to Rebeck, "He persisted in his position and went on to explain that male playwrights somehow, innately, are able to transcend their gender and write about the human condition, while women playwrights, also innately, are not."

She was cautioned early on not to let herself be "ghettoized" as a woman playwright. The implication: Women who identify themselves as "women playwrights" are not likely to see their plays produced in major regional theaters or on Broadway.

Because she is someone who does not follow the ways of the crowd, Rebeck rebelled against that warning and initially dismissed it as implausible. But she later wrote that "my work, which at the time I considered to be fairly straightforward comic realism, was increasingly being branded as 'feminist.' People thought I was making a big political statement; mostly what I was really trying to do was write what I knew, which was what it means for this one person (me) to be a woman in the late twentieth century in America."

WHAT IS FEMINISM?

Feminism can mean a number of things. Historically, in the United States, it has meant women seeking rights and freedoms that they are entitled to as human beings. It has also meant that women wish to obtain all the opportunities available to men.

The first feminist movement in the United States arose around the middle of the nineteenth century and lasted until 1920, when American women finally won the right to vote. This "first wave" of Feminism was defined by women wanting access to higher education; the freedom to work outside the home; the right to sign contracts, own property, and divorce their husbands if they chose; and the right to vote in local, state, and federal elections. This first feminist wave achieved many of its goals.

The "second wave" of Feminism occurred in the United States toward the beginning of the 1960s and continued until the early 1980s. Once again, it was a movement seeking specific rights and freedoms. For instance, women wanted access to the kinds of jobs for which men are traditionally hired, and women wanted equal pay for equal work. More controversially, women wanted the same sexual freedom that they believed men were allowed to have. Women also wanted the right to make choices about reproduction, including the choice to have an abortion. In 1963, Congress passed the Equal Pay Act (EPA), and in 1973, the Supreme Court decision entitled *Roe v. Wade* made abortion legal.

Feminism also influenced women who wanted to work in theater but felt that commercial show business, particularly Broadway, was a man's game. As the excellent historian Charlotte Canning describes in her book *Feminist Theaters in the U.S.A.*, for about fifteen years — from around 1968 to 1983 — women all over the country founded theaters for and about women: At the Foot of the Mountain, The Women's Project, Lilith, Spiderwoman Theatre, Split Britches — and many more.

This was also the period that saw the emergence of the first post–World War II generation of female playwrights: experimenters such as Maria Irene Fornés, Megan Terry, and Rosalyn Drexler, and, hot on their heels, the more mainstream trio of Marsha Norman, Wendy Wasserstein, and Beth Henley. Groundbreakers all.

But the passion and determination of second-wave feminists eventually ran up against political conservatism. In the decades since the Equal Pay Act, women have had to go to court to enforce their right to equal pay. More than forty years later, a woman in the United States earns only seventy-eight cents for every dollar a man makes. The Supreme Court's *Roe v. Wade* decision continues to draw opposition from members of the pro-life movement.

Second-wave Feminism spurred an ever-growing number of female playwrights and directors. But as Canning documents, by 1990 most of the companies founded by women had folded, victims of dwindling public and private funds for what many considered agenda-based organizations.

These issues, and the mistaken assumption that feminists are strident protesters who do not like men, gave Feminism a bad name. By the time Rebeck started her playwriting career in the late 1980s, the general public regarded Feminism as a cause to be avoided, or even dismissed.

REBECK'S VIEW OF FEMINISM

Ironically, while the male theater establishment was perhaps recoiling because Rebeck wrote feminist plays, feminists were also chastising her, but for a different reason. A number believed she was showing women in a bad light.

The misunderstanding of Rebeck's work on both sides is apparent from the critical reaction to her third major play, *Loose Knit*, which opened Off Broadway at Second Stage Theatre on June 30, 1993, directed by Beth Schachter.

Set in a Manhattan apartment and an upscale Japanese restaurant, *Loose Knit* involves five women, purportedly friends, who gather once a week to knit. One of them — the sole married woman among the five — secretly arranges dates for the other four, in each case with the same nasty but very rich and good-looking man. Ultimately, the single women wreak a kind of revenge on both the arrogant date and their married friend, whose husband is having an affair. The play closes, however, on a note of reconciliation among the women.

The play received a rave review from Stephen Holder of *The New York Times*, but despite that positive response, Jeremy Gerard, reviewing for *Variety*, believed that neither the men nor the women in the play exhibited any redeeming qualities, and he just didn't like the play, period. Feminist critics meanwhile found fault with a script that showed women betraying women and one needy female after another allowing a misogynist to debase her.

Both responses miss Rebeck's point. "I still believe," she said during an interview this author conducted with her in 1999, "that part of what Feminism has to accomplish . . . is to give us permission to make the kinds of mistakes that men are allowed to make. . . . Female characters should be allowed to be as big a mess and have as big of a struggle as anybody. I think that Feminism hasn't gotten us anywhere until we are given permission to find ourselves and make mistakes the way men can. That's where the power is. I'm also," she added, "not interested in girls who are right."

The women and men in *Loose Knit* are both "right" and "wrong." They have their messy, ugly sides and their generous, likeable aspects.

Miles, the obnoxious seducer, comes close to being a one-dimensional villain, but even he has moments of insight about the women he treats so appallingly. As in many of her plays, Rebeck writes characters that are alive with contradictions. The women collude with their oppressor even though they hate being with him. The husband loves his wife, but most of the time he cannot stand the way she behaves. "We're all in the soup together," Rebeck has said. Her characters are multifaceted human beings.

That, in fact, is how Rebeck defines her personal brand of Feminism. "I do think of myself as a feminist," she once told this author. "I was so sad that it became kind of a dirty word, because I don't think Feminism is about anything other than women being as fully human as men. I thought the idea was to erase the bigotry that says we have certain roles to fill. I thought it was about teaching us to see each other as complicated human beings who have choices. That's what Feminism has always been to me."

This attitude, which is reflected in Rebeck's first three full-length plays, makes her work challenging to direct, watch, and critique. On the page, Rebeck's characters shift believably among a range of outlooks, changing their minds in reaction to other human beings' behavior the way characters in a novel tend to do. We may yearn for definite heroes and villains. But people are not one or the other, Rebeck keeps reminding us. There are at least ten sides to most human beings. There are no sure answers or clean resolutions — only choices.

TWO CHEERS FOR HOLLYWOOD

In 1990, Rebeck married Jess Lynn, a production stage manager whom she had met at Brandeis. That year she also began writing for television, specifically for a string of situation comedies that included *American Dreamer*, *Dream On*, and the CBS TV series *Brooklyn Bridge*.

Rebeck, like many American playwrights, sought out TV assignments because she and Lynn did not make enough money in the theater to survive. In New York, Rebeck was "temping" — working a temporary job — at AT&T, and her husband was working two shows at once, and still they were living on the edge financially. She recalls coming home one evening to find Lynn collapsed on the couch, too exhausted to get up and say hello. Then and there she decided that she had to find a writing job in Hollywood. If she didn't, they would have to quit the theater.

As Rebeck wrote in her book *Free Fire Zone: A Playwright's Adventures on the Creative Battlefields of Film, TV, and Theater,* at first, working in television was about as close as she had ever come to a waking nightmare. The power games were merciless, the egos outlandish, the end result — the writing itself — usually compromised to the point where it could not even be called writing. Money was the only compensation that made the horror worthwhile, even for a lowly story editor like Rebeck.

She worked for *Brooklyn Bridge* for about a year and a half, with Lynn staying in New York and flying back and forth to Los Angeles. But then she was fired. The way Rebeck interpreted this outcome, *Brooklyn Bridge* producer Gary David Goldberg let her go because she had "not respected his power enough." She had used the wrong tone of voice or dared to argue with Goldberg about the nature of some of the characters, particularly the women. Whatever the actual reason for the dismissal — Rebeck always put it down to her challenging Goldberg's authority in some way — she was out. Next stop: the 1992 situation comedy *Here and Now,* produced by Bill Cosby for Warner's. But she was fired from that show, too, when a consultant erroneously blamed her for a script that introduced a white female character into the largely black series.

So Rebeck moved back home to New York, Lynn, the theater, and scraping by. Eventually, she would write for television again and gain much more personal satisfaction from the experience, but first she transformed her Hollywood nightmare into vivid comedy.

POWER PLAYS

Out of her first serious encounter with commercial television emerged a new direction in Rebeck's dramaturgy: plays about seeking, taking, and holding power.

The Family of Mann, based mostly on Rebeck's stint for *Brooklyn Bridge*, received its premiere in New York, directed by Pamela Berlin at Second Stage Theatre and opening on June 28, 1994. The autobiographical central character, a smart, educated writer named Belinda, experiences the kind of culture shock that Rebeck endured while navigating the treacherous waters of a TV writers' room.

Not that Rebeck leaves sexism behind. Far from it. The sexism of the male producer and the male director is hilariously blatant, from graphic language to clumsy seduction attempts, from the way they treat the black, female production assistant (who must hop-to when anyone wants coffee) to the fictional world of their retro sitcom, *The Family of Mann*.

But the sexism is part of a larger picture: the Machiavellian ploys by which these men and almost everyone else working on this sitcom power their way past weaker colleagues. The only goals in the world of Rebeck's play are to make more money, secure more status, and wield more authority than anyone else, male or female. The neophyte Belinda arrives on the scene imagining that everyone wants to write a good situation comedy. She quickly learns that the only standard is to win.

In *Family of Mann*, Rebeck departs from her realistic style. There are hints of absurdism as the action moves from the writers' room to the sitcom, where the writers take the roles of parents and grown children and scenes occasionally build to a maniacal frenzy. Toward the play's end, Rebeck delicately introduces a poetic, absurdist note. Clara, the production assistant, is one of the few good-hearted characters in the play, and after she, like Belinda, loses her job, she sprouts a pair of angel wings, which only Belinda can see. In the City of Angels, Rebeck suggests, things are topsy-turvy. Loathsome people like Belinda's executive producer rule the world, while a well-meaning person like Clara is out of work.

Reviewing the production for *TheaterWeek* magazine, this author wrote that Rebeck was "adept at dramatizing the competitive interplay" among the characters. David Richards, then chief drama critic for *The New York Times*, wrote, "Power is all that counts in this world [of the play]. If you're not in a position to humiliate somebody, you're nobody."

On September 13, 1996, slightly more than two years after *The Family of Mann* opened, New York Theatre Workshop produced *A View of the Dome*, Rebeck's satire on power, Washington, D.C. style.

"What I like about *A View of the Dome*," this author wrote in *TheaterWeek*, "is that Theresa Rebeck plays around. She'll go along, writing in a satirical but logical way, and then all of a sudden she'll launch into farce, or make a 90-degree turn that feels unrelated to the plot. She's not afraid to go out on a whimsical limb stylistically, with the result that this cynical take on political life in the nation's capital both surprises and entertains."

The action takes place in a restaurant frequented by politicos and kingmakers. Here, one night, a well-known academic dines with a coterie of Washington insiders who persuade him to run for a Senate seat. Pushed to the side, at a table alone, sits a young woman named Emma, who is actually responsible for the man's imminent rise.

In earlier plays like *Sunday on the Rocks* or *Loose Knit*, Rebeck might have sent Emma to her female friends to argue the pros and cons of avenging this rejection. But after the sojourn in Los Angeles, Rebeck's plays reveal a more suspicious attitude about power and a new willingness to dramatize its aggression. Emma begins the play as an idealist supporting a potentially great candidate. But as she watches him lose his moral center, she too wades into the Washington fray, destroying and being used in turn. "Emma," Rebeck agreed, "becomes no better than the rest." Well, almost no better. She becomes a mother at the end of the play and acquires an awareness of her mistakes. "There's something about having a child," said Rebeck, "that pulls her back from the brink."

REVISITING TELEVISION AND LIKING IT

Perhaps Rebeck was injecting an autobiographical note into *A View of the Dome*, for in 1995 she had given birth to a son, Cooper. That year, Rebeck had also been asked to write an episode for *NYPD Blue*, Stephen Bochco's gritty TV series about the rough-and-tumble world of a New York City police squad.

In contrast to her experiences with sitcoms, she felt that writing the *NYPD Blue* episode was "pretty wonderful." The episode was shot the way Rebeck wrote it. The series was only in its second season, and it was a hit, so everybody still brought enthusiasm to the work. Handsome, intense Jimmy Smits had just joined the cast, and he was a strong actor, worth writing for.

But when Rebeck was offered a job on the *NYPD Blue* writing staff, which would mean moving again to Los Angeles and reentering the Hollywood scene, her first inclination was to say no. Her husband, however, urged her to accept, because he perceived that she would never receive a better offer. They kept their New York apartment, rented a furnished house in Los Angeles, and moved. Lynn stayed home with their son during the day while Rebeck worked on the show, an arrangement that pleased both of them and continued even after they returned East. Rebeck has said that she finds doing it all — being artist, mother, and family breadwinner — "exhausting and stressful."

She stayed with *NYPD Blue* for two years, garnering a Mystery Writers of America Award and a Writers Guild of America Award for

Episodic Drama. But after two years, she felt it was time to move on to other TV series, new films, and especially theater. "I get crazy if I go too long without working on a play," she once said.

MISTRESS OF THE ONE-ACT PLAY

"For the contemporary playwright," writes Christopher Burney in his introduction to Theresa Rebeck's collection of one-act plays, "short plays too often become the forgotten jewels of a body of work."

During the first decade of her playwriting career, audiences and critics largely knew Rebeck's talent through her full-length plays produced at regional and Off-Broadway theaters. But she had also become an inveterate and skilled writer of one-acts, a number of which were produced at Naked Angels West in Los Angeles.

In some respects, the one-act form is harder to write than the so-called full-length play. The short form demands a tight structure and focused action. It allows for no waste but requires a well-modulated internal pace, or else the action feels contrived. Ten-minute plays have become a staple of certain festivals in recent years. But generally, the American professional theater turns up its nose at one-acts, even though some of its finest writers, notably Tennessee Williams, Maria Irene Fornés, and Sam Shepard, have produced superb examples of the genre.

Rebeck's one-acts are funny, perceptive gems about urban society. Burney, associate artistic director of Second Stage Theatre, which has produced some of Rebeck's major work, writes that her one-acts "reveal a mind carefully attuned to the rhythms of our society and a deep understanding of the personal obstacles individuals face." Set in bars, restaurants, bedrooms, subway cars — locations that are instantly recognizable and require minimal furniture onstage — her realistic short plays quickly establish character, relationships, and conflict. They provide an opportunity for Rebeck not only to wield her satiric pen but also to express the dark side of her vision, for while she may poke fun at her characters' foibles or miseries, she cannot help but reveal the bleakness of their situations as well.

The Actress, which takes place on a beach where two out-of-work performers have gone to escape the ferocious competition for acting jobs, is about an actress so obsessed with missing a possible audition that she cannot talk about anything else — or enjoy the beach.

In *The Contract*, Rebeck cleverly inverts the power struggle between a desperate actor and his agent. The actor, Tom, begins the play in the all-too-familiar position of beggar, trying to persuade his agent, Phil, that he can do anything: "I also dance," he coaxes, and "I don't really see myself as a type. There's much more range . . ." But finally Tom threatens to walk out of the office, and Phil suddenly becomes the needy one. End result? A contract!

Josephina also contains an unexpected ending. This one-act — actually a monologue — is Josephina's memory of living through the Holocaust. For most of the brief play, you think she is talking as a Jewish victim who survived. Then, in the last two or three minutes, she reveals that she survived by betraying Anne Frank's hiding place to the Nazis.

Rebeck's one-acts feel as though they were written effortlessly, but they are expertly crafted slices of contemporary life. Each has a beginning, middle, and end. The action is clear and strong. Often the climax of the action is a complete surprise, but it is the sort of revelation that is believable and gives an audience pleasure.

"I like this short form for how much it resembles a fist," said Rebeck. "You have to get so much done so quickly, in terms of laying out stakes and character and language, and you have no time to meander. You just have to drive those little plays forward until they smash into the place that they are going."

PORTRAIT OF A WORKING PLAYWRIGHT

In the span of ten years, from 1988 to 1998, Theresa Rebeck had become one of the country's most prolific dramatists. She had seen five major plays and an adaptation (of Eugene Ionesco's *Rhinoceros*) produced either in the regions, Off Broadway, or both, and *The Family of*

Mann had been a finalist for the 1994–95 Susan Smith Blackburn Prize. She had written numerous one-acts, many of which were produced, and had become a respected writer of prime-time TV drama. She had written the screenplay for *Harriet the Spy*, produced by Paramount Pictures and Nickelodeon Movies and released in 1996 (it was the first Nickelodeon movie). Based on a 1964 novel by Louise Fitzhugh, this delicate mingling of comedy and drama focused on an eleven-year-old aspiring writer who takes notes on everyone and everything she sees.

Rather than feeling overwhelmed by the demands of writing in different media, Rebeck seemed to thrive on it. She had also learned a huge amount about the different ways that language and time work in theater, television, and film. And, very significantly for the development of Rebeck's style, she had validated for herself the importance of storytelling — a skill owned by the writers she always admired most, like the great nineteenth-century English novelist Charles Dickens. "I love his exotic language," said Rebeck. "His abundance of characters, the dazzling narrative skill, and the powerful moral center. I love the way the enormity of his spirit enters into every corner of those novels. I love the fearlessness of his compassion for all his characters."

In *Free Fire Zone*, she writes that not every playwright cares about storytelling, nor every director. She cites a comment by a "famous director" who once scoffed that a good yarn is "so boring. All that story, it makes the audience so *happy*. It's all so *dreary*."

Rebeck believes that a well-told story should be at the heart of any good drama, whether in theater, television, or the movies. Not plot, which she defines as "when things just happen," but story: the emotional thrust beneath the plot. "Story," Rebeck writes in *Free Fire Zone*, "is when a character is compelled out of some deep need to act, and those actions result in events, good or bad, that affect that character's journey and the journeys of others. The story rises out of this morass of humanity like an inevitable song. That is story."

Or, as she passionately told the sneering director, "Story is like a cup. . . . It's the cup that holds everything. Everything we do — is made possible by the story. If we don't have a cup, everything just spills all over the place."

But just as when she was a youngster, Rebeck's inclination to speak her mind got her in trouble. Like the eleven-year-old heroine of *Harriet the Spy*, who is briefly victimized when she loses her notebook and her observations about her schoolmates are revealed, Rebeck drew fire for calling things as she saw them.

After her first Hollywood stretch, she said, "You know, it's not like I intend to be a gadfly, but my gut reaction is to say, 'Come on, guys, this is nuts.' I think that everybody else is going to go, 'She's right. It's nuts.' But people are thinking other things as well, and they're not excited that I'm saying it. . . . My instinct is to peel things apart. It's one of those things that is particularly difficult for the culture to accept from a woman."

Rebeck became a kind of lightning rod for the ongoing discussion about whether women who write plays receive equal treatment with men from American theater producers, artistic directors, and critics. Rebeck had no qualms about citing what she saw as the American theater's lapses on that score, or addressing what she believed was the critics' tendency to suggest that her playwriting had been damaged by her TV work. As she saw it, that complaint felt like another way for critics to dismiss women. "Critics are always looking for ways to take women's authority as writers," she once said. "There's a cultural unease with women having creative authority." In response to a 1999 *New York Times* article, "Unlocking Broadway: Outsiders Seek the Key," Rebeck wrote a feisty letter to the editor, which ran on June 13, 1999:

> While American playwrights have a right to wonder why their work isn't more often represented on Broadway, I wonder why it is seen as "at best distracting and at worst damaging to their craft" to make a living writing for television or the movies. . . . American playwrights should be permitted to

make a living without being accused of selling out. Writing for television and the movies is potentially no more damaging to one's craft than sitting around a tiny apartment and stewing over why you're broke.

Rebeck is actually fairly objective about how writing for television affects her dramaturgy. She is alert to the possibility that, because a writer has to work so quickly for a TV series, one can become "facile with language." In addition, the realistic nature of television means that "you pretty much write the way you hear people talk." She sees positive aspects to that but also the danger of losing theatricality. When moving from television back to theater, "I had to recommit to letting language take the stage more." In television or film, where the camera can focus tightly on an actor's features, the raising of an eyebrow or the twitch of an actor's mouth often communicates more than words. "Sometimes," said Rebeck, "you don't need speech, because of that eyebrow." The stage, however, relies on words as well as spectacle. "There is more room on the stage," Rebeck explained, "for a fullness of language. More room for language to fulfill a larger destiny."

But she also believes that writing good television taught her valuable lessons about writing plays. Speaking during a 1999 interview about *NYPD Blue*, Rebeck said, "I had to move things forward on two levels all the time. I had to move the plot forward and the characters forward. I could have characters moving in different directions, but every scene had to move something forward. There wasn't a stillness to it. And I actually found that to be a powerful way of storytelling. But finally the theater is not so single-mindedly reliant on momentum. There should always be forward movement, but you do in fact have more time, more leeway, to let language perform."

During the next decade of her career, Rebeck's plays would continue to explore language, style, and new themes.

SEEKING NEW TERRITORY

Unsurprisingly, perhaps, artists are fascinated by artists — by how the artist is made, how she or he creates and survives in a world where so many people do not understand or value artists. As Rebeck approached the millennium, she wrote two plays in which artists figure prominently: *Abstract Expression*, which opened November 13, 1998 at the Long Wharf Theatre in Connecticut, staged by Greg Leaming, and *The Butterfly Collection*, which Playwrights Horizons opened Off Broadway October 2, 2000, with Bartlett Sher directing.

In *Abstract Expression*, the artist in question — an aging, alcoholic Abstract Expressionist painter named Kidman — finds his dormant career suddenly springing to life when a New York gallery owner rediscovers his work and arranges an exhibition. Kidman, who has been impoverished, surviving only because his daughter, Jenny, earns a meager living and takes care of him, now stands to make millions of dollars from the sale of his paintings.

A happy ending? Not really. The play is filled with ironies. For one thing, although Kidman is apparently a talented painter, he is also one of the most unpleasant people around — dirty, foul-mouthed, selfish, and verbally abusive toward his daughter. Anybody who comes to this play assuming that artistic talent equals personal grace is in for a surprise. And Kidman is ruthlessly practical. Although Jenny abhors the prospect of public attention and acquiring money that is going to change their lives radically, her father has few qualms.

In yet another ironic twist, Kidman dies before he can enjoy any of his fame and fortune. At the end, the gallery owner gets her retrospective, and Kidman's son, Willie, gets the money. And Jenny, who truly worshipped her father's talent, is left with only one painting by which to remember him.

Abstract Expression did not come into New York, but it has had a life in the regions ever since.

SURVIVING THE CRITICS

Abstract Expression explores how one artist can bring turmoil to his family. The *Butterfly Collection* presents a whole family of artists and art lovers. Paul, a famous novelist, is struggling to prepare a manuscript for his publisher and hires a young, aspiring fiction writer named Sophie to work with him. On hand at Paul's home in Connecticut are his wife, who has spent her life attending to her demanding husband; their sons Frank, an antiques dealer with a fine eye for rare items; and Ethan, a self-absorbed actor; and Ethan's girlfriend.

As in *Abstract Expression*, the central figure is a despicable person. By the end, we are pretty certain that Paul's wife has written large portions of the books for which her husband is famous, and that Paul has also borrowed from Sophie's manuscript about her grandfather, who collected butterflies.

But where *Abstract Expression* leaves us with the view that the art world is grasping and meretricious, *The Butterfly Collection* presents a range of perspectives and, in that respect, is a richer play. The antidote to Paul is Sophie, who may never be recognized publicly but is truly an artist (even Paul sees that). What is an artist? In Rebeck's vision, the artist is sometimes a fake, often mediocre, and just occasionally, quietly and beautifully, the real thing.

It is one thing to receive weak notices "out of town." It is quite another to face them in New York City, especially when a dramatist knows that regional theaters look to Broadway and Off Broadway for plays. The public dousing that Bruce Weber gave *The Butterfly Collection* in *The New York Times* on October 4, 2000, astonished even Rebeck, who has low regard for critics to begin with. Noting that the two male artists in the script — the novelist and the actor — were egomaniacs and that all the female characters suffered at their hands, Weber condemned the play for being "agenda-based writing." At the end of the review with gratuitous unpleasantness, he complimented the male director for making the production happen at all, considering that the female playwright must have resented him from start to finish.

Rebeck writes in *Free Fire Zone* that *The New York Times* review killed regional productions of *The Butterfly Collection*. For a time, it also seemed to kill Rebeck's playwriting career, or so she felt. She grieved and retreated into a private realm of humiliation, pain, and anger. But as she advises in *Free Fire Zone*, that is not a healthy place for an artist, and she recounts amusingly that "after . . . drugs, alcohol, therapy, behavior modification, meditation, going to the gym, . . . not going to the theater . . . and not reading the *New York Times* . . ." she regained equilibrium. She and her husband also adopted a daughter, Cleo, who had been born in Heifei, a city in the Anhui province of China, on November 19, 2001, and left on the doorstep of an orphanage when she was one day old.

Rebeck's work was not seen in New York City for more than three years after the closing of *The Butterfly Collection*. Then *Bad Dates* arrived on June 3, 2003, at Playwright's Horizons, in a production staged by John Benjamin Hickey.

Written for the marvelous Julie White, who had become something of a muse for Rebeck — she had appeared in *Spike Heels* at Second Stage Theatre in 1992, and acted Belinda in *The Family of Mann* — *Bad Dates* is a bit of a throwback to Rebeck's earliest comedies about the female condition. "We had been friends for a long time," Rebeck said about White, "and we talked about working on something together. She was dating at the time, and I thought the stories of her dates gone awry were charming and relevant. I also, for several years, had been interested in writing a novel, and I was insecure about knowing how to do it. So my brain figured that if I tried my hand at novel writing by giving myself a first-person narrator, I could write a novel by pretending that it was just a long monologue. Then I thought, 'But I've never written a really long monologue.' *Then* I thought, 'Well, I could write a one-woman show: that would be good practice for writing a novel.' And it was."

A one-person play, *Bad Dates* begins with Haley (White) trying on shoes and clothes — preparing for a date — and talking to the audience.

As the play moves along, we learn about Haley's experiences being a single mother and about her career managing a restaurant and about all the awful dates, blind and otherwise, on which she goes. A jolt of theatrical adrenaline arrives when Haley informs us that her restaurant managing is not completely above board and that the shady characters who own the restaurant might be coming after her —— a plot twist that deepens character and leads us to an unexpected place at the end. Indeed the play takes us on a hilarious and touching journey into one woman's chaotic world. It also provides a glorious turn for an actor, as many a performer has discovered, for *Bad Dates* would end up receiving many regional productions from California to Texas to Arkansas, and continues to be produced today.

Three months after *Bad Dates* opened, Ben Brantley, the chief *Times* drama critic, reviewed *Omnium Gatherum*, a dark, post-9/11 comedy set at a dinner party in hell, which Rebeck had written with the playwright Alexandra Gersten-Vassilaros. Brantley admitted that he had gone to the play anticipating "a glib intellectual lampoon." Instead he witnessed "a piping hot slice of satire."

Rebeck and Gersten-Vassilaros had written *Omnium Gatherum* directly after terrorists attacked and destroyed the World Trade Center on September 11, 2001. The play's march toward production was fairly speedy: A reading took place at The Actor's Studio in March 2002, followed by workshops during the spring and summer at New York Stage and Film, and another workshop at Naked Angels in New York in January 2003. Less than three months after that, *Omnium Gatherum* received a full production directed by Will Frears at the Actors Theatre of Louisville; during the annual Humana Festival of New Amerkcan Plays, and on September 25, 2003, a production staged by Frears opened Off Broadway in a commercial house.

The play was selected for *The Best Plays Theater Yearbook 2003–2004*, and Chicago theater critic Chris Jones, who had admired the play in Louisville, wrote in his essay for the volume that "During those trying months [after 9/11] there developed a general sense that a mature, complex, globally savvy, daring and smart play — directly about the terrorist attacks and our tough new world of homeland security — had still to be written. *Omnium Gatherum* is the first of those plays. One could make a case that it's still the only one."

To Rebeck's delight, the play was nominated for the 2004 Pulitzer Prize for Drama, and although the award went to Doug Wright's *I Am My Own Wife*, Rebeck could legitimately feel that her reputation as a playwright had been vindicated. She had climbed back into the ring.

FIRST LOVE: MELODRAMA

Studying nineteenth-century melodrama had long ago planted an urge in Rebeck to write an all-out, no-holds-barred melodrama, or at least adapt one. Around 1999, she had embarked on a musical version of Adolph d'Ennery's *Les Deux Orphelines (The Two Orphans)* with the composer Kim D. Sherman and colyricist John Sheehy. The popular nineteenth-century French melodrama, which had been the source for D. W. Griffith's famous 1921 silent film, *Orphans of the Storm*, dramatizes the trials and sacrifices of two orphaned sisters, one of whom is blind. The original is set in post-revolutionary France; Rebeck and her collaborators transported the story to New Orleans after the Civil War, and made the sisters former slaves.

But Rebeck had difficulty finding a venue for the musical until Brandeis University gave it a student production in December 2005. She had more success finding a professional slot for *The Bells*, which McCarter Theatre Center produced on its main stage beginning March 22, 2005; directed by McCarter's artistic head, Emily Mann.

The history of this melodrama begins in nineteenth-century England, when the British dramatist Leopold Davis Lewis translated a French play, *Le Juif Polonais*, and renamed it *The Bells*. In 1871, the British actor-manager Henry Irving produced the play and starred in it, in a performance that brought Irving fame as an actor of great psychological truth. Set in Alsace, the melodrama involves an innkeeper named Mathias (Irving), who must confront a murder from his past and wrestle with issues of guilt and justice.

Rebeck told McCarter's dramaturg, Liz Engelman, that she was fascinated by the way the original play "used the stage picture to portray interior states of mind," and she thought about that Expressionist approach for a long time before beginning her adaptation in 2001. She moved the locale to Alaska circa 1899 and 1915, approximately the time span of the Yukon gold rush. Alaska stirred her because of its beauty, coldness, darkness, and mystery. The gold rush, she told Engelman, attracted her "because of how desperate a situation it was. . . . Those men really looked into the mouth of hell, to go up there and get that gold. And I am still pondering the mystery of that." The combination of the locale and the story sparked Rebeck's imagination and spurred her "to make sure that I have landed the world of my play solidly within an American identity."

Forging an American identity for the play also inspired director Emily Mann. For Mann, a dramatist in her own right who has written what she calls "plays of testimony" about events and issues in twentieth-century American history, Rebeck's adaptation represented "an extraordinary American story . . . about greed, about the need for money, about committing murder and living with that by living in a state of denial." Mann saw parallels with contemporary American society.

Mann gave the play a remarkable production. Scene designer Eugene Lee's black-and-white landscapes evoked snowbound Alaska, and Frances Aronson's "spectral" lighting heightened the Expressionist moods that Rebeck wanted to create. Rebeck found the experience enlightening. For one thing, she told Engelman, "I don't often get to see my work brought to life on such a grand scale." And vitally for Rebeck as a playwright, she was able to explore the relationship between melodrama and epic — the point at which an emotionally charged tale becomes larger than life and universal.

WRITING LARGE

Pursuing that exploration, Rebeck moved forward with *The Water's Edge*, her version of Aeschylus' tragedy *Agamemnon*, set in contemporary New England. It opened June 15, 2006, at Second Stage Theatre's elegant space on West 43rd Street, staged by *Omnium Gatherum* director Will Frears.

Agamemnon had been the opening salvo in Aeschylus' great trilogy, *The Oresteia*, about the aftermath of the Trojan War. At the end of that seventeen-year conflict, the Greeks, led by their general Agamemnon, defeat the Trojans, burn their city, and enslave the Trojan women. Agamemnon, who has sacrificed his daughter Iphigenia so that the Greeks can be victorious, comes home with the Trojan princess Cassandra in tow.

But while the general has been away fighting, his wife, Clytemnestra, has taken a lover, Aegisthus. And when her husband returns, she stabs him to death in his bath and murders Cassandra, too.

Interviewed for *BOMB* magazine by the producer and theater professor Evangeline Morphos, Rebeck spoke at length about what led her to transfer this ancient story to contemporary times.

> I was hoping to reinvestigate the Greek model of *Agamemnon*, where trauma is not something anyone seems to be able to recover from. They do their best to boldly push through what's happened in the past . . . but it's impossible for them to do that. And I thought for all their involvement in ritual and religion, those Greeks were pretty acute about human psychology as well. I reread *Agamemnon* — I check in with the Greeks periodically—and I was looking at the Oresteia trilogy thinking, there's all this commentary about the return of the king and the *ownership* of the kingdom, but isn't this about the fact that he killed his daughter?

In Rebeck's reconception, Helen (Kate Burton) and Richard (Tony Goldwyn) have been separated for seventeen years — ever since, because of Richard's inattentiveness, their young daughter drowned in the lake that we see just beyond the house. When the play begins, Richard arrives unexpectedly, accompanied by a youthful girlfriend (played in the original production by Mamie Gummer, Meryl Streep's daughter). He has some inkling that he can atone for his long-ago carelessness, but Helen's grief and rage still swirl within her. And whether she has been planning her revenge these seventeen years (Rebeck's view); or whether the idea of murdering her husband occurs to her soon after he appears (Burton's interpretation); toward the play's end, she stabs him to death in a discarded bathtub in her yard.

Morphos praised Rebeck's gutsiness, her willingness to write boldly and theatrically, and Rebeck responded that "I'm not interested in small theater anymore." But, as she explained to Morphos, that did not necessarily mean writing metaphorically or nonnaturalistically. "For me," said Rebeck, "*theatrical* means strong. *The Water's Edge* comes off as startling because it's strong; it's surprising; there's disturbance in it. People were really rattled by the play on a deep psychological level. That is, to me, theatricality."

Nearly three years later, on February 3, 2009, the London production opened at Arcola Theatre, a fringe venue in Hackney, that often stages variations on classic plays.

"Chilling;" "brilliantly staged," and "bursting with passion, revenge and trance-like poetic speeches," were some of the responses that greeted Rebeck's United Kingdom debut.

BROADWAY BOUND

There were few critical doubts about *The Scene*, which had its premiere in March 2006, at the Humana Festival of New American Plays and then opened in New York at Second Stage Theatre on January 12, 2007. Both productions were directed by Rebecca Bayla Taichman.

In many ways, the play is a coming together of what is best about Rebeck's playwriting. There is the sharp ear for contemporary conversation. There are contradictory characters that elicit both admiration and disgust. There is the theme of men objectifying women and female characters either suffering angrily or responding in kind. There is verbal wit, farce, and the sort of humor that emerges from a character's behavior.

In addition, *The Scene* — like all good comedies of manners — paints a scathing picture of a segment of Manhattan's show-business world, represented by Charlie, a continually out-of-work actor; his wife, Stella, who books talent for a TV talk show; their friend Lewis, who does not seem to do much of anything but makes enough money doing it; and Clea, the sexy, seemingly innocent new girl in town who leaves destruction in her wake. As Stella says about Clea with true Rebeck wit, "She looks good in black and can't speak the English language. She'll do just fine in Manhattan."

To be sure, *The Family of Mann* had skewered the sort of people who ferociously vie for success in commercial television. But *The Scene*, perhaps because it dramatized a less specific group, conveyed a universal message about the state of contemporary life in a glittering American city where trawling for contacts at parties can be a major occupation. The ending of *The Scene* is also considerably bleaker than that of the earlier play. Wifeless and broke and ditched by Clea, who has used him and moved on, Charlie turns up at one of those parties, a homeless man on the outside looking in.

Rebeck, in an interview with Mervin P. Antonio for the Humana Festival, summed up the worldview that the play embodies: "We're culturally far, far adrift from what we meant to be as a country," she told Antonio. "I think there is a cultural collapse into narcissism that has not been fully examined. It makes the world more and more surreal."

Charles Isherwood, reviewing the Off-Broadway production for *The New York Times*, wrote that "Ms. Rebeck's dark-hued morality tale contains enough fresh insights into the cultural landscape to freshen what is essentially a classic boy-meets-bad-girl story. The doomed Charlie is seen as both a victim of, and a symptom of, a morally corrupt culture."

By 2007, Theresa Rebeck had been writing plays for almost twenty years, and the best of America's young directors had staged her work. She had been produced at every level of the American theater — except Broadway.

To those who keep track of such things, this, perhaps, is not a surprise. The number of plays by women that are produced on Broadway is far below the number written by men. More women write for the American theater now than at any time in the country's history, but Broadway remains an unattainable venue for most of them.

That all changed for Rebeck when the not-for-profit Manhattan Theatre Club (MTC) and Boston's Huntington Theatre Company coproduced *Mauritius* on October 4, 2007, at the Biltmore Theater (now the Samuel J. Friedman Theater), a restored Broadway house that MTC had acquired. It was the sole new play by a woman to be produced on Broadway during 2007–08. (Broadway's only other play by a woman that season was a revival of Caryl Churchill's *Top Girls*.)

The title *Mauritius* refers to a pair of rare stamps from a small island country in the Indian Ocean, part of a collection that has been left to two half-sisters. According to an interview she gave Robert Simonson in *The New York Times*, Rebeck was surfing the Internet one day and discovered a soon-to-be-auctioned stamp collection belonging to a Spanish lord. She thought the stamps were beautiful, began to explore the culture of philately, and discovered that stamp collectors are completely obsessive. "It became clear," she told Simonson, "that there was some kind of hunger in these people that the collection of objects answered. I found that mysterious and moving."

In the play, the younger sister, Jackie, wishes to sell the stamps; the older sister does not. There are also three philatelists of varying degrees of greed and criminality who would be happy to get their hands on the precious items. The women's personal conflict lends the drama some gravitas, but there is no question that the most enjoyable part of *Mauritius* — the part that makes you sit up in your seat and hang on every word — involves who is going to wind up with those stamps. As Rebeck said about writing for *NYPD Blue*, "There's something about crime drama that my little heart responds to." If creating suspense is any indication of a writer's skill — and it is — Rebeck's heart was clearly relishing the story and plot twists of *Mauritius*.

The Huntington had given the play a reading and subsequently its world premiere in October 2006, staged by Rebecca Bayla Taichman. The critical response was positive enough to garner IRNE (Independent Reviewers of New England) Awards for the play, the production, Eugene Lee's set, and Marin Ireland's performance as Jackie. The Boston theater community's Elliot Norton Awards recognized the "outstanding" production and actor Michael Aronov.

By the time *Mauritius* opened on Broadway a year later, however, the creative roster had changed. Tony Award–winner Doug Hughes had replaced Taichman and assembled his own team: John Lee Beatty was on board to design the set, Alison Pill was playing Jackie, and Aronov was gone. The star F. Murray Abraham headed the cast.

Hughes, whose Broadway résumé includes the Pulitzer Prize–winning, *Doubt*, and a recent revival of *The Royal Family*, adored the play's theatricality. "I loved the opportunity to work on a story that had the twists and turns of a beautifully constructed thriller," he recalled. "It's a caper story with a great emotional life that holds its own against all that wonderfully inventive plot. I thought it was just marvelous that Theresa would write a play reclaiming territory that long ago was conceded to the screen. It's her *Maltese Falcon* or *The Big Sleep.*"

But over at the paper of record, Ben Brantley called the play "deftly formulaic." He distinguished between the production, which he liked, and the writing, about which he had doubts. Like other critics, he felt compelled to note that the plot contained what he believed were echoes of David Mamet's 1975 opus *American Buffalo*, in which three small-time crooks try to steal a rare buffalo nickel and fail abysmally. Unlike the critics who thought Rebeck was simply imitating Mamet, Brantley at least understood that she was purposely toying with Mamet by adding "estrogen to a testosterone base." Still, while acknowledging "the pleasurable kick of watching a woman . . . take on a slew of Mamet-esque thugs," Brantley finally decided that "the angry passion that has illuminated much of Ms. Rebeck's work, . . . flickers only occasionally here."

Was Rebeck channeling Mamet? Or was she playing with his style and his characters' famously macho attitudes, as in her 1992 one-act *What We're Up Against*? In that funny, mocking play, Ben and Stu sit in their office sharing a bottle of scotch and dissing a female colleague. The griping and cursing, the derogatory terms for their absent coworker, and the half-finished sentences sound straight out of Mamet's *American Buffalo* and *Glengarry Glen Ross*.

"Of course David Mamet is an influence on my work," Rebeck explained vehemently to this author. "The real question is, why is this an issue? All writers are in relationship with other writers who came before them. Why is what I do seen as inappropriate? Is there rhythm in my language? Yes. Do I curse well? Yes. Did Mamet influence me? Sure. I don't know any writer of my generation who hasn't been influenced by him. Other influences on my work are Molière, Chekhov, Ibsen, and Shakespeare. Structurally and comedically and psychologically, my work is much more influenced by those writers, with whom David Mamet has historically had very little traffic. I do not believe the focus on Mamet as a singular influence is accurate. Frankly, I think the critics are mostly shocked that a woman curses as well as I do. And I say, to hell with them on that account. They can just catch up with reality. I'm not a lady. I'm a playwright."

Whatever the reason, the majority of the city's most visible critics refused to let down their hair and have a good time at *Mauritius*, which closed after only sixty-one performances. As Hughes put it, "From the first preview on, audiences were enthralled by the play. Some of the cultural mandarins appointed to tell us what's good and what's not classified it disparagingly as 'melodrama.' But I am reminded of what [film director] Billy Wilder said: 'Ah, melodrama. That's what the snobs call it when the audience cares what happens next.'"

Beyond New York, critics would prove less straitlaced. *Mauritius*, like so many of Rebeck's plays, secured a second life in regional theater. The successful 2009 production at San Francisco's Magic Theater breathed new life into that struggling venue. Robert Hurwitt, the long-time drama critic for the *San Francisco Chronicle*, on June 3, 2009, called the play an "Ingenious, ferociously funny and emotionally dynamic crime caper," and Bob Verini, reviewing the Pasadena Playhouse production in *Variety*, on April 6, 2009, called it a "Heartfelt musing on loss, regret and entitlement; it's an altogether exciting, richly rewarding experience." "The work draws you in with its twists and turns . . . *Mauritius* ensnares us in the tricky pursuit of genuine value," wrote Charles McNulty in his April 5, 2009, blog entry at the *Los Angeles Times*.

AN ESTABLISHED PLAYWRIGHT

Since the Broadway debut of *Mauritius*, Rebeck has seen two more new plays produced Off Broadway. *Our House*, a satire about the TV industry that involves an ambitious anchorwoman who willingly becomes the hostage of a deranged fan, received its world premiere at The Denver Center Theatre Company in January 2008. Slightly over a year later, on June 9, 2009, Playwrights Horizons gave *Our House* its New York premiere, directed by Michael Mayer. *The Understudy*, a backstage farce with hints of darkness about a talented stage actor who is understudying a not-so-talented film star on Broadway, opened November 5, 2009, at the Roundabout's Laura Pels Theatre, directed by Scott Ellis and with a star-laden cast: Mark-Paul Gosselaar, Justin Kirk, and Julie White.

Terry Teachout, in *The Wall Street Journal* on November 6, 2009, gave *The Understudy* what is called "a rave" in show business. "Farce is the trickiest of theatrical genres," he observed, "but the first half of

'The Understudy' is a little masterpiece of comic clockwork in which the craziness mounts steadily from scene to scene. . . . Harry's opening monologue, in which he marvels at the inexplicable fact that 'talent-free' actors . . . are paid millions of dollars to dodge phony bullets and scream lines like 'Get in the truck!' on camera, says just about all that will ever need to be said about big-budget action films." Teachout urged The Roundabout to move the production to Broadway. Production and play — part backstage romp, part acid commentary on America's flaccid cultural values — proved popular with audiences.

THERESA REBECK AND THE AMERICAN THEATER

Today, Rebeck is one of the most widely produced dramatists in the United States. In April 2003, when she received the Otis Guernsey New Voices Award from the William Inge Theatre Festival, the festival's artistic director, Peter Ellenstein, noted that "her work has been appearing more and more frequently on America's stages and she is helping to inspire younger writers throughout the country." Indeed, Rebeck enjoys mentoring emerging writers, and lends her expertise to the Lark Play Development Center and the Mentor Program at the Cherry Lane Theatre.

Adventuresome as well as skilled, Rebeck is an artist who apparently follows where inspiration leads — whether to theater, television, film, or narrative fiction. In 2008, Random House published Rebeck's first novel, *Three Girls and Their Brother.* Set in New York, it tells about the grandchildren of a famous literary critic, three of whom — the girls, who all have naturally red hair and are drop-dead gorgeous — suddenly find themselves tangling with show business and fame, challenges with which Rebeck is definitely acquainted.

Many dramatists shy away from writing novels. Susan Glaspell (1876–1948), was one of the few American writers who could pen both a best-selling novel and a Pulitzer Prize–winning drama (*Alison's House,*

1930). Anita Loos (1888–1981), who gave the world that unique hero-ine Lorelei Lee, of diamonds-are-a-girl's-best-friend fame, was another American adept in both forms. A novel often demands lengthy descriptions, an interior narrative voice, and several actions unspooling over the course of several hundred pages. A play usually involves one tight action and dialogue, rather than description or lengthy narrative.

But Rebeck's first encounter with the genre is a pleasurable, jazzy, page-turning journey into the highs and dangers of celebrity, with a good dollop of satire. Reviewer Diane White, in *The Boston Globe*, called *Three Girls and Their Brother* "pointed and funny, an entertain-ing, cautionary story about the powerful and preyed upon." Melissa Rose Bernardo, in *Entertainment Weekly*, wrote that "Playwright Theresa Rebeck is known for black comedy and hyper-intelligent heroines, and both figure in her first novel . . . a frizzy satire of celeb-obsessed NYC." *Vogue*, certainly no stranger to the world about which Rebeck is writing, decided that "Rebeck delivers a crackling exposé so dead-on it's arguably closer to social realism than satire."

Random House is publishing Rebeck's second novel, *Twelve Rooms with a View*, in 2010, and has contracted with her for two more. It will be stimulating to see how, or if, Rebeck's narrative fiction interacts with her playwriting, both artistically and in terms of her career.

The Novelist, in fact, is the new title of *The Butterfly Collection*, the play whose critical reception in 2000 hurt Rebeck so deeply. She has rewritten the script and hopes to see it receive new theatrical life. As she explained to this author, "I felt that [Sophie's] monologues at the beginning and end confused the focus of the piece. I very much think that the play's psychological motor and focus is the story of Paul and Ethan, which is a morass of rage and disappointed love. I wanted it to stay clear that Sophie is truly a pawn between them — she is not a victim, but she is a pawn. So I reworked the shape of Act Two to make that clear. There is an honored tradition of building a new play out of an old one. *Summer and Smoke* became *Eccentricities of a Nightingale*. If it's good enough for Tennessee Williams, it's good enough for me."

Definitely Rebeck is a model for anyone, man or woman, seeking a successful example of dedication, persistence, and earning power in several of the world's chanciest professions.

She does find each discipline disheartening at times and says so. "I don't really like writing movie scripts," she wrote this author. "I would love to make a movie some day the way John Cassavetes or Woody Allen does — come up with a script for actors you have worked with and like, and see what you can construct from the talents of people who trust and respect each other. The studio culture, and now much of the independent movie culture, is not terribly interested in writers. It's very interested in directors and stars and big, glorious images. In both film and television there is so much interference from executives, it's hard to gather to yourself enough authority to be the ultimate voice of the story. Everyone wants to pick at it. That happens less in theater, although it's not like it never happens in the theater. Plus, my experience is that real craziness enters the process when the critics show up. They often feel to me like studio executives with notes from another planet. In all three forms people who really don't have anything to do with the storytelling process interfere with the transfer of the story from the storyteller to the audience. Now that I'm writing novels as well, I find a sort of blessed simplicity in the transfer of the story to the reader."

That "transfer of the story from the storyteller to the audience," is an element of theater that Rebeck particularly savors. Perhaps that is one reason why she is enamored of Victorian melodrama. Nineteenth-century melodrama reached across the footlights to the audience. Plays demanded that theatergoers engage with moral questions, and audiences often responded loud and long to the action onstage. Rebeck believes that theater should be pleasurable as well as meaningful. "I feel a playwright can entertain and also say something about the culture and about human character."

Rebeck's stylistic range has expanded since she first began writing plays to include melodramas, musicals, and mysteries, as well as comedy. Her satiric range has also enlarged. She began by focusing on the inequities in male-female relationships, and moved to indicting American politics and that preposterous cultural phenomenon — the American TV industry. Along the way, she has delved deeply into writing about theater itself and artists in general.

Rebeck's strength remains her acute awareness of the language and behavior of men and women navigating the rocky shoals of urban existence. Her ability to dramatize their conflicts and confusion, their anger and occasional moments of joy — and to amuse us while doing do — distinguishes her art and her contribution to contemporary American theater.

It is often helpful to look at a playwright's work in the context of who has come before. In Rebeck's case, that means going back to Rachel Crothers' plays from the first two decades of the twentieth century to find another female playwright who comically and pointedly discloses sexism in male-female relationships. But Crothers (1878–1958) possessed a streak of sentimentality; Rebeck does not. Crothers did, however, see her major plays produced regularly on Broadway, and Rebeck, so far, has only broken through that glass curtain once.

Among female playwrights who have come to the fore since the second wave of Feminism, it is tempting to compare Rebeck to Wendy Wasserstein (1950–2006). Wasserstein — three of whose major plays were produced on Broadway — wrote comedies, and is frequently cited as a dramatist who explored the conflicts experienced by contemporary women.

But Rebeck has more styles at her command than Wasserstein and a more trenchant worldview. Rebeck truly is a theatrical gadfly, often landing where other playwrights, male or female, do not dare to go, and biting through our complacent social skin. She is that invaluable theater artist, a playwright who combines sharp social vision with populist flair. She is also a stellar example of how far women who write plays have journeyed since the women's movement of the 1960s and 1970s. Their determination, faith in their own possibilities, and independence of spirit live today in Rebeck and her exceptional body of work.

DRAMATIC MOMENTS

from the Major Plays

These short excerpts are from the playwright's major plays. They give a taste of the work of the playwright. Each has a short introduction in brackets that helps the reader understand the context of the excerpt. The excerpts, which are in chronological order, illustrate the main themes mentioned in the In an Hour essay.

from **Abstract Expression** (1998)
from Act One, Scenes 1 and 2

CHARACTERS

Charlie
Sylvia
Eugene
Phillip
Lucas
Lillian
Jenny

[The play begins with a monologue from an impoverished man named Charlie, who will turn out to be a loyal friend of the Abstract Expressionist painter who is one of the central characters. Scene 2, an example of Rebeck writing comedy of manners, takes place at a dinner party, where the cater-waiter, Jenny, turns out to be the daughter of a once-famous, but now reclusive, Abstract Expressionist artist. A gallery owner at the dinner party decides to visit the artist, to see his work and consider it for her gallery.]

SCENE 1

Lights up on a man at a table. He is unloading a bag of groceries and talking to a small bird in a cage on top of a very small television set.

CHARLIE: Who needs money? Long as we can eat and watch a little television now and then we be OK, hey sweet pea. Look at this, dollar ninety-nine for toilet paper, you believe that? Plus they raised the coffee again, I don't really care long as I don't have to drink that stuff tastes like nuts and berries. Four ninety-nine a can. That's a crime. If I was making the rules, I'd keep down the coffee, that's what I say. Only sure way to stave off the revolution. Yeah, don't look at me like that, I got your peanut butter. *(He pulls it out of the bag and looks at it.)* Reduced fat. They charge the same and take things out, that's the way the world, huh. Everything just shrinking down, well, we don't mind. You and me and a good cup of coffee, little television, who needs money. Like a kingdom in here. *(He looks at his mail and stops at a letter. Considers it, then goes back to the can of coffee.)* Make me some coffee. *(He studies the can. Blackout.)*

SCENE 2

Lights up on a dinner party. Eugene, Sylvia, Lillian, Lucas, and Phillip are finishing their dessert and coffee.

SYLVIA: I just think the whole thing is much ado about nothing. I mean, the city has been going to hell as long as I can remember, I just think it should go there in style and I'm not going to apologize about that.

EUGENE: Don't be ridiculous Mother.

SYLVIA: I'm not being ridiculous, it's absolutely everywhere in the news again. The gaps between the rich and poor, as if this were a noteworthy situation, or an actual social condition or something. When it's really nothing more than a definition. I mean, it's just what the words mean, isn't it? Some people are rich, and some are poor, and the poor ones don't have as much money. How is this news? This is some idiot's idea of news.

LILLIAN: Sylvia. You're just trying to be controversial.

SYLVIA: But I'm not! This isn't even original, what I'm saying. I mean God, people have been — who was it who said that thing about poor people being around all the time —

PHILLIP: The poor will be with you always?

EUGENE: That was Jesus Christ, actually.

SYLVIA: There, that's what I mean. Even he was saying it and he liked them.

(Jenny enters and starts clearing plates.)

LUCAS: Your point being what, Sylvia? I mean, I'm not saying I disagree with you, but this is starting to make me uncomfortable. I am a person of color after all —

SYLVIA: Oh don't start that. That's not what I'm talking about and you know it. I'm just saying how bad is it really, being poor? Don't you think they're exaggerating, at least a little, the source of all our social problems et cetera, et cetera, well I know plenty of rich people who have social problems. And if the rich are as bad as the poor, socially I mean, or any other way for that matter, well. Then all this fuss is really over nothing.

EUGENE: All what fuss? I don't even know what you're talking about.

SYLVIA: You do, too, and don't use that tone with me, young man.

EUGENE: I'm not using a tone, Mother, you're just rattling on about nothing as usual —

SYLVIA: *(Overlap.)* Oh really, and may I say your manners are lovely, at your own engagement party, which I am paying for I might add —

EUGENE: Oh for God's sake —

SYLVIA: Well, honestly, you're turning into one of those people who hate their own money and I don't have anyone else to leave it to —

EUGENE: Mother —

LILLIAN: Eugene does not hate money. I won't let him.

(She kisses his hand.)

EUGENE: *(Good-natured.)* Of course I don't hate money, that's ridiculous. I'm just uncomfortable with the assumption that just because you have it that means you know something about social conditions.

PHILLIP: Well why shouldn't it mean that?

EUGENE: When in fact I happen to know that she personally has never spoken to anyone whose trust fund is smaller than two mil on a good day in the market.

SYLVIA: Oh that's not real money —

LILLIAN: *(Laughing.)* Sylvia —

EUGENE: *(Animated.)* Meanwhile we live in a city where people are

starving, literally starving, if the newspapers are to be trusted
at all —

PHILLIP: Which they're not —

SYLVIA: Oh, nobody starves on Manhattan. Manhattan is thirty-four
square miles of room service, my father used to say that.

(They all laugh.)

EUGENE: Not that I care, I don't care. I just don't know why you keep
going on about it.

SYLVIA: Oh, now you're upset.

EUGENE: I'm not upset.

LILLIAN: What about you, are you poor?

*(She looks at Jenny. Jenny stops her cleaning for a moment and looks up,
surprised.)*

PHILLIP: *(Amused.)* Oh really, Lillian.

LILLIAN: What's it like?

EUGENE: Lillian.

SYLVIA: Oh no, that's not what I meant at all. I don't want to know what
it's like, that's not the point.

LUCAS: No, I think it is.

(Jenny starts for the door, carrying plates.)

LILLIAN: Where are you going? I asked you a question.

JENNY: *(Surprised.)* Oh.

LUCAS: You're serious.

LILLIAN: Eugene has a point. I don't see how we can talk about this,
consider ourselves informed on any level, if we're not willing to confront the reality of poverty in the city.

(To Jenny.) So what's it like? Can you tell us?

SYLVIA: Yes but she's not poor. Look at her, she's clearly educated.
You're educated, aren't you, you're an actress or something.

LUCAS: Actresses are poor.

JENNY: I'm not an actress.
SYLVIA: But you're educated.

(There is an awkward pause at this.)

JENNY: I've been to high school.
SYLVIA: Not college?
JENNY: No.
LILLIAN: But you graduated high school.
JENNY: *(A slight beat.)* I haven't, actually. Excuse me.

(She heads for the door, with the plates.)

SYLVIA: Oh, you dropped out, is that it? To be an actress, or something?
EUGENE: She already said she's not an actress, Mother.

   (To Jenny.) I'm sorry. You need to finish up, and we're keeping you.
SYLVIA: All of a sudden you're so sensitive, well, she can just answer
   the question before she goes. What is it like to be poor?

(They stare at Jenny. She considers this.)

JENNY: It's like not having enough money.
SYLVIA: This is my point . . .
JENNY: You worry a lot.
SYLVIA: You worry? Well I worry.
EUGENE: You worry about your nails, and whether or not you can get
   theater tickets.
JENNY: Did you need anything else?
LILLIAN: Stop trying to run off, this is interesting.
JENNY: It's not interesting. It's not. It's just, you don't have enough
   money. That's all it is. You skip breakfast. You buy cheap shoes. You
   stand in the drugstore and try to figure out how much it costs per
   aspirin if you buy the big bottle instead of the little one, and all you
   can think is of course it's better to just spend the money and have the
   big bottle because then you've paid less per aspirin, but if you do
   that, there won't be enough left to go to a movie and sometimes you

just want to go to a movie. You'd be amazed at how long you can think about that. Then you think about other cities where movies don't cost eight dollars and you get mad, 'cause eight dollars is a lot, for a movie, it's . . . It's boring, really. A lot of boring things stick in your head for a long time. You just, you think about money all the time.

EUGENE: *(Dry.)* So in one way at least, it is like being rich.

SYLVIA: Don't your parents help you?

JENNY: My mother's dead.

PHILLIP: What about your father, doesn't he work?

JENNY: No, he does work, he works very hard. But he's, actually, he's an artist.

LILLIAN: An artist? You mean a painter?

JENNY: Yes.

SYLVIA: Oh, that's different. Her father's an artist. So she's poor, but it doesn't count.

EUGENE: Why not?

SYLVIA: Artists are supposed to be poor. It helps their art. And don't argue with me about this, I'm right about this.

LILLIAN: *(Interested.)* What's his name?

JENNY: Walter Kidman.

LILLIAN: Mac Kidman?

(There is a surprised stir at this. Jenny is clearly startled.)

LUCAS: *(Amused.)* My God, Lillian. You know this man?

LILLIAN: Is it him?

JENNY: *(Now truly uncomfortable.)* Yes, actually.

LILLIAN: No one's heard from him in years. He's still painting?

JENNY: Of course he's still painting. That's what he is, he's a painter.

PHILLIP: *(To Lillian.)* Is he any good?

LILLIAN: There was some debate about it, but he had something of a career, what, fifteen or twenty years ago. My uncle reviewed one of

his shows. He didn't much like that particular batch, but he always
felt he had talent.

JENNY: Your uncle?

LILLIAN: Yes, he was the art critic for the *Times*. You must've been a
child, I'm sure you don't remember.

JENNY: Of course I remember. It was his last show.

LILLIAN: Was it?

JENNY: I have to go.

(She suddenly turns and heads for the door.)

LILLIAN: *(Calling.)* But your father's still painting?

JENNY: *(Tense.)* Yes. He is.

LILLIAN: I'd love to see what he's doing these days. I have a gallery.
Lillian Paul. My uncle had terrific respect for your father. He just
thought he was going down the wrong track, I think.

(A beat. Jenny doesn't respond. She finally turns and goes.)

SYLVIA: Well, that was rude.

EUGENE: For God's sake. You were examining her like she was some
kind of bug!

SYLVIA: We were expressing interest. How is that a bad thing?

PHILLIP: This Kidman was good, you say?

LILLIAN: Not likely but for God's sake you can't say that to the man's
daughter. What kind of a bitch do you think I am?

(They laugh. Blackout.)

****

from **The Actress** (2002)

CHARACTERS

Mike

Nina

[Theresa Rebeck's mastery of the one-act form is revealed in this tight comedy about an actress and actor who go on a vacation to escape the rat race of their profession. Except that, try as she might, the actress cannot relax — to the despair of her companion.]

Mike and Nina walking on a beach. Mike carries a lot of stuff. Nina is looking for a good spot.

NINA: This looks great. Right here. Is this great or what?

(Mike sets the stuff down. Nina moves five feet to the left.)

NINA: *(Continuing.)* Wait a minute. This is . . . no wait. *(Moving to the right again.)* No wait. Right here. No wait.

MIKE: Nina!

NINA: Right here, that's what I'm saying, right here.

(She starts to take her wrap off, five feet from where Mike is. Resigned, he picks up all the stuff again and moves to the spot she's picked.)

NINA: *(Continuing.)* This is incredible. The ocean? I mean, it's incredible, right?

(Without waiting for a reply to anything, she just continues to talk, while Mike unloads.)

Oh, you were so right. This was just what I needed, just a break from everything. Four days at the beach, it's just brilliant, you know, absolutely, the sound of the waves, I mean, that is a meditation all it's own. A meditation. Sun. Water. Birds. You'd have to be nuts not to see the beauty in this. It's so relaxing.

MIKE: I told you.

NINA: That's what I'm saying, you told me and you were right, I said you were so so right. *(She slathers suntan lotion on herself, talking.)* I mean, I did not want to do that stupid workshop. That play just sucked, yet another opportunity to play some idiot doing things that make no fucking sense whatsoever, for no money, that no one is ever going to produce. I mean, someone should put these poor playwrights out of their misery. Who fucking needs it.

MIKE: This is better.

NINA: Please! Are you kidding? Look at this! I so needed this. After that pilot season, oh my God, you know they keep saying this is the worst one yet and then the next one is just worst. It's like how do they keep getting worse? But they do! It's so fucking demoralizing.

MIKE: Nobody got anything.

NINA: Nobody got anything! Who are they hiring anymore? It's like they go out and look and look and look until they find the worst actors out there and then they're the ones they give all the jobs too!

MIKE: It sucks.

NINA: It so totally sucks.

MIKE: This is better.

NINA: This is so totally better, are you kidding? Because I am just completely disgusted with it. I mean, I didn't even get close this year. Last year at least I got close, that cops and public defenders in Manhattan show, I almost had that, but no they had to hire a movie star . . . oh shoot. Why am I thinking about that again? Six callbacks. I thought I was going to have heart failure.

MIKE: They do that to everybody.

NINA: *(Suddenly vulnerable.)* No, I know, I just . . . you know how when something that disappointed you just comes up again, all of a sudden? Oh, shoot. On such a pretty day? Why does that happen? I thought I was over that. *(Beat, sad.)* I really wanted that. I would have been good in that.

MIKE: It didn't make it on the air anyway.

NINA: *(Putting the lid back on it.)* Thank God, that script was just the stupidest thing I ever read in my life. And that cow they hired, please God help me, she can't act her way out of a paper bag, that's why her movie career dried up! I mean, does it make sense to hire someone who is a total fucking failure as an actress, just because she was bad in a couple of movies in her twenties?

MIKE: You want to take a walk?

NINA: No, I'm relaxing, this is so relaxing, just being here. Don't you think this is relaxing?

MIKE: Yeah. No, yeah.

NINA: I am so relaxed. Those fuckers. Those fuckheads. Who fucking needs it. I am a fucking artist, I do not fucking need this kind of fucking rejection every day.

MIKE: Nobody does.

NINA: I know. Fuckers. This is so relaxing.

(She leans back in her chair, looks at the sky. Mike listens to the roar of the waves. Nina shifts in her seat.)

NINA: *(Continuing.)* And I was not going to do that workshop anyway. That play is idiotic.

MIKE: Nina.

NINA: I mean, how many fucking bad plays can you do before you just get completely fucking demoralized?

MIKE: I know but you know. I mean. You know?

NINA: Because fuck.

MIKE: You want a soda or something?

NINA: I would love a soda.

MIKE: Here.

(He gets a soda for her out of the cooler, gets one for himself. She opens it, takes a drink, looks around. He does the same.)

MIKE: *(Continuing.)* God, that tastes great. You know, that is a damn good fucking can of soda. Sodas on the beach. Sometimes I am really just grateful. Because this is . . . I mean, life is . . . I mean, look at that stupid bird. That is so beautiful. Look at him, just . . .

NINA: Oh yeah.

MIKE: Right?

NINA: Fuck yes. This was a fantastic idea, coming out here. As opposed to what, hanging around the city and doing some loser workshop of a bad play, this is a no fucking brainer.

(Mike nods, not knowing how to respond.)

MIKE: This is a good soda.

NINA: I mean, I'm an actress. You know? I am an interpretive fucking artist. Give me something to interpret, why don't you, then you'll see something. All I ever do is audition for shit, total shit, that's all anyone is doing anymore. Television, film, the theater, all of it, it's completely unwatchable.

MIKE: Maybe you should take some time off. I mean, maybe that would actually be good for you.

NINA: What is that supposed to mean?

MIKE: I mean . . .

NINA: You mean stop?

MIKE: No no, that's not what I mean. I just mean, I don't do it anymore and it's fine.

NINA: What do you mean, you don't do it?

MIKE: Come on, Nina, I don't — I mean, I don't do it. I haven't been on an audition in five months.

NINA: It was a shitty pilot season, everyone knows that.

MIKE: That's not what I mean.

NINA: No one got anything.

MIKE: Listen, I don't feel bad about it. You don't have to make me feel better.

NINA: I'm not.

MIKE: It's just, I don't know. I think I decided that I like being a bartender. The people come in and talk to you, it's interesting. They all do so many different things, and you know, you're a bartender so they want to talk to you. And I realized that every time somebody told me what they did, I'm a lawyer, I'm a real estate broker, I work in a shoe store, I'd say, yeah, I'm an actor. Like I wanted to let them know that I wasn't really a bartender, I was really not what it looked like I was. And everybody was always really nice about it. But it just hit me one day that I was being kind of dumb. To be spending your life thinking that what you were doing wasn't real, like you're just doing that while you're waiting to do something else with the rest of your life? So for a couple days, I did this experiment, whenever people told me what they did, I said, I'm a bartender. That's what I told them. I'm a bartender. And it felt kind of good, you know. It actually did. I like being a bartender. I like not thinking about what I'm not all the time.

NINA: Everybody needs to take time off once in a while.

MIKE: I'm not taking time off. I'm a bartender. I'm a bartender, sitting on a beach.

NINA: Well, I don't know how to respond to that.

MIKE: You don't have to respond.

NINA: So, what, you want me to say, I'm a caterer sitting on the beach?

MIKE: That's not what I'm saying.

NINA: No fucking way. I think I'm a little better than that. If you don't mind.

MIKE: That's not what I'm saying.

NINA: I don't know what you're saying.

(A beat.)

MIKE: It's just, I thought it would be good to get away.

NINA: I said it was, what have I been saying?

MIKE: I know you have, I just . . .

NINA: I should have done that workshop.

MIKE: No, come on.

NINA: There were a lot of people coming to see that. After the shitty pilot season I just had, I cannot afford to just turn down work.

MIKE: Come on, Nina. That's not what I meant, at all.

NINA: Well, what did you mean? You meant I should just admit I'm not an actress —

MIKE: No —

NINA: I should just give up my entire identity —

MIKE: No, come on —

NINA: Well, I'm just not ready to do that all right? I still have a dream of being an artist. I'm not going to apologize for that and I'm not going to just give it up. It's the best part of me. I can't just give that up.

(Beat.)

MIKE: Don't do it. Come on.

NINA: I'm sorry if you don't understand that.

MIKE: I do understand that, Nina —

NINA: I am not giving up everything I have worked, you know how hard I work —

MIKE: Yeah but, that's what I'm saying. We can —

NINA: Maybe it never meant the same thing to you.

MIKE: OK maybe it didn't but you do. You do, and and a baby —

NINA: I just can't be asked —

MIKE: Come on, honey. Come on. I think we should have it —

NINA: Do you know what it does to your figure? It's hard enough to get work. It's hard enough.

MIKE: I can take care of us. I love you. Come on. I love you.

NINA: That's not the point. *(Beat.)* Is this why you asked me to do this? A couple of days away at the beach so you could, you could hound me about this?

MIKE: *(Beat.)* I just thought it would be good to get away.

NINA: *(Beat.)* I should have done that workshop.

(She cannot look at him. Blackout.)

(End of Play)

****

from **Bad Dates** (2003)
from Act One, Scene 1

CHARACTER

Haley

[In this funny one-woman play, Haley — a restaurant manager and single mom in her late thirties or early forties — talks to the audience about her life: her dates, bad and good; her experience running a restaurant; and, finally, the crisis that ends the play. In Scene 1, she is getting dressed for a date and occasionally running down the hall to talk to her (unseen) teenage daughter.]

A woman, Haley, stands alone, in her bedroom. It is a friendly, warm space, not frilly. There are clothes thrown everywhere, and a lot of shoes, a very very lot of shoes, although the shoes are not in piles. She handles them with some care.

HALEY: Do you like these shoes? They're cute, right?

(Dissatisfied, she throws them down and goes to pick through several pairs that are on the bed. She starts to put them on.)

I can't wear shoes anymore. You know, it's not that you can't wear them, but you start to go, oh God these things hurt, they're kind of like some medieval Japanese perversion.

(She goes down the hallway, calls.)

Vera! Hey, come look at these. Come on, it's a big night for me.

(A doorway open, the sound of teen music, Haley yells over it.)

Do you think these are cute? I mean — these are cute, right? You're right, you're right. They hurt, anyway.

(The music stops as Vera's door is shut. Haley hobbles back into her bedroom.)

Listen, I haven't looked at these things in years. It's not like I have a fetish or anything. I mean, I know that it looks like I have a fetish. Well, I do have a fetish, but it's not like some crazy Imelda Marcos fetish, although I admit it might look like that.

(She looks at a pair of shoes in a box, then shows them to the audience.)

These aren't as cute as I thought. Joan and David. Remember when you thought they were cute, and now they're not, they're just not hip enough? It's 'cause the name isn't good enough, that's what I think. Jimmy Choo, much cuter name and sure enough the shoes are cute in a timelessly cute way.

　　(Off the dagger-like heel.) Well, maybe not cute. They look like you could stab someone with this heel, don't they, what is that about? Anyway, I used to live six blocks from this shoe store in Austin, George's shoe store, I kid you not that was the name, not very glamorous, the name or the store, which was kind of a little dump but this guy George had some sort of a deal with all these major shoe designers and he got their leftovers, which he sold at rock-bottom prices out of this icky little hole in the wall. This place was a miracle. Everything he sold was something like twenty or thirty bucks, I am dead serious, you could go down there at least once a week and pick up a three hundred dollar pair of Chanel pumps for a mere thirty dollars. Well, you couldn't do that every week, that only happened to me once, but it was an unforgettable day, as you may imagine. Here they are . . .

(She holds them up, jubilant.)

OK. A little conservative but still unspeakably chic. Thirty bucks. But you had to have the right size foot. Six to seven and a half, that was mostly what he sold, that's mostly what the leftovers were, your foot's bigger than that you are mostly out of luck. I took one of my friends there, she's a size nine, she had to go outside and have a good cry. Anyway, the other cool thing about this astonishing little store, there was a lady's spike heel shoe, huge, it was like size eleven or something, and someone had glued little macaronis all over this shoe, and then spray painted it brown, and it was in the window. It looked like something a kid would have done, and then to be nice, his dad put it in his store window. So I was very touched by this shoe, even though the color it was spray painted was kind of icky. If you're going to go to all the trouble with the macaroni, wouldn't you think to paint it lime green, or sparkles or something? Anyway — oh ow. Oh no. This can't be . . . oh no . . .

(She has on the Chanel pumps, which are too tight.)

Dammit, they shrank. Shoes don't shrink. My feet grew. Oh shoot. They're not that cute anyway. Yes, oh yes they are. Oh I'm going to just weep. Shoot. Maybe I'll just frame them, or something. Anyway this shoe store, you just couldn't resist —

(She opens a box and, surprised, sees a huge wad of cash.)

Oh wow, well, this does not belong with the shoes now does it?

(She packs it back up and puts the shoebox under the bed.)

Anyway, I ended up with some pretty strange shoes, I'll admit, zebra stripe half boots, gold lame spikes, you know, stuff you just think is too wild to pass up, maybe the occasion or the outfit will someday present itself. And George was nice, and I'm moved as I said by the shoe with the macaronis. So I end up with this huge collection of shoes for very little money. And I was pregnant. The two things really didn't have much to do with each other, although I'm sure I was wearing something in this mess the night Vera was conceived. Whatever. So the next thing I know I have six hundred pairs of shoes, a husband — Roger — and a kid. And then things start disappearing around the house, including the Toyota, which Roger has traded for three pounds of marijuana. I hope you don't think ill of me for admitting all this. Because I am not that person anymore, having a child makes some of us grow up. Not all of us, Roger being the relevant case in point. I'm going to weep I am just going to weep, do none of these fit? What kind of cruel universe would do that to me? So the next next thing I know I'm a divorced waitress with a five-year-old kid — see these are cute, and they fittttt.

(She looks at herself in the shoes in the mirror.)

Yeah they're cute, of course they're cute, they belong to my daughter. I look like a thirteen-year-old in them. *(She starts to take them off.)* *(Yelling to door.)* Hey, I found your blue buckle shoes!

(She sets them in the hallway, shuts the door.)

Anyway, we move to New York, Vera and I. Fresh start. We're in the big city, getting by, you know, I got a nice little job as a waitress. I found this amazing apartment — rent-controlled! And things are looking up, definitely, when it turns out this restaurant I'm working at is some kind of front, some Romanian mob put all their money in it as a tax shelter or money laundering, I can't even, believe me, you didn't want to know, at that point I was raising a five-year-old and the less I knew about —

(She starts in on another pair, very high heels.)

I'm mostly hoping the Feds or the police or whoever don't find out whatever illegal activity is going on, because I don't want to lose my job. Then sure enough — ow, God, ow —

(She walks around.)

OK, these hurt but they fit.

(She continues to walk, looks at herself in the mirror.)

I'm sorry this story is taking so long. Because it's just of course the police do figure out something — I think it was money laundering —

(She starts to change her clothes, into a snaky little dress.)

— Which I of course suspected, as I said, and then have to lie about when all these detectives descend and ask how much you know. I felt like such a terrible person. They had this whole complicated sting worked out, one of those things that they spent years setting up, so you know they've been working for years figuring out something you knew all along. But you can't really feel sorry for them because why the hell did it take them so long? Besides which they're being kind of pushy and snotty around the restaurant, making us all wait in the back, where there's no place to sit, and not telling anyone what's going on, my little girl is with her babysitter and I'm not even allowed to call, and all of us, we're all like great, there goes my job, and finally I say to one of them, the cops, What's going on, anyway? And he's like, some big macho, when we need to talk to you, we will let you know. And there is so much creepy attitude, I mean, this is our lives he's messing with and he's just some big old nasty cop. So I say to him, look, is this about the money-laundering thing? And he sort of looks at me, all surprised, and says Oh you know all about that, huh. And I said, well, isn't it common knowledge?

At which point one of the cooks offers me a cigarette, just to get me to shut up. I mean, I admit I was being a bit stupid, they had already taken Veljko off in handcuffs. We all of course felt that it was about time somebody did — Veljko was just a big fat criminal, there was no question, big and fat and mean, he looked like Al Capone or a cardinal or something, and it was a huge relief someone finally arrested him, but my point is, this was clearly a serious matter, I had no business mouthing off to anybody.

(She looks at herself in the mirror.)

OK, that looks good. Right? This is very good. I look like a hooker. Well, maybe I can wear this with a scarf. You know, look like a hooker wearing a scarf or something.

(She starts to look for a scarf.)

So then, all the guys who are running the restaurant are completely arrested but then the family, which as it turns out not all of them, apparently, are mobbed up, you know how those things work, there's always like a couple who are not complete criminals but they can call up the complete criminals when they need a favor. So that side of the family decides to keep the place open, but they have no idea how anything works, so I'm the one ends up walking them all through it night after night 'cause I'm apparently the only one who knows anything about how the place works. Everybody else there is so concentrated on their own little piece of turf no one knows anything about the whole place, except me. So, you know, the noncriminal Romanians finally go to hell with it, and put me in charge, because apparently I'm sort of weird restaurant idiot savant. Who knew? Born to run a restaurant. Which is exciting. When you find something, some strange combination of, who you are and what you can do, to find your gift like that? How many people get that to fall on their head like that? 'Cause I started out being like just a waitress trying to support herself and her kid, I mean I was just another person who married a moron and then had a load of shit to deal with.

(Off outfit, in mirror.)

Yeah OK, this is a clear disaster but I do like the top.

(She starts to take off the skirt.)

So things are swinging. I'm allowed to do things that nobody else ever thought of, add stuff to the menu, change the layout of the place and get rid of the lousy flatware, you know, plus I went out and stole somebody's chef, not the nicest thing I've ever done, but they were abusing him over there, I mention no names, but chefs are artists. You treat them nicely.

And the next thing I know — 'cause this stuff happens so fast you can't even, you would not believe and I mean that — we get reviewed in *The New York Times*, it's a rave, and Leonardo DiCaprio throws his birthday party at my restaurant and we are on Page Six!

And business goes through the roof. Which could not be more fun. So I'm feeling fantastic, because there is nothing better in life than being allowed to do a job that you're good at, so guys are asking me out all the time. I mean I am *en fuego*, and I don't actually have time to date, between the restaurant and Vera, so I'm turning them all down, which makes 'em want me even more! But I'm thinking, there's got to be a way to work this out, I miss sex, it would be fun to have someone to talk to, besides Vera, who is a great kid but let's face it she's seven by that point and I'm hitting my sexual prime. So I'm contemplating this, I'm ready, there's this guy hanging around who seems like a good possibility, you know, he's nice, and funny, and great looking in this skinny way. You know how great looking skinny guys are sometimes? So he's showing up three or four nights a week, just to have a drink and flirt. And this is very high-end flirting, you know, when he says something snappy, and you hand it right back to him only better and then float away to show somebody to their table, and then curve back around the bar for another dazzling four-second encounter, it was sooo dreamy, and he finally asks me out, and I am yes yes yes. I mean, I like this guy, I really — He — whatever. The thing is, right then — right then, this friend of mine, Eileen, sees this Joan Crawford marathon on some movie channel. And she comes over the restaurant laughing her fool head off, and says have you seen Mildred Pierce? 'Cause Haley, it is you. She thinks this is this big hilarious blinding insight, cannot stop laughing, so I rent the video. You know, I go out, I rent the video, and I watch it.

(Haley looks at the audience. Beat.)

OK. Have you seen Mildred Pierce? Joan Crawford, gorgeous, competent, devoted to her kids, husband turns out to be kind of a loser, so she goes out and gets a job — as a waitress. She's got no training, does it because she has to, and turns out to be — well, you know, kind of a restaurant idiot savant, gets her own place, it's a huge hit, she doesn't have time to date but men are falling over her so she finally starts to date them and terrible terrible things happen, and everything goes to shit. I mean, I am not making this up. That is what happens in this movie I truly, I mean, oh Lord. And oh, get this. The kid's name? She has an evil daughter? Veda. My kid's name is Vera. And they are nothing alike, Vera is really a good kid, she's more like the tragic daughter who dies, but still. I mean! On top of it, this guy who's been sniffing around, asking me out, is just a dead ringer for Monty, the evil socialite who Mildred marries and who steals from her and then destroys her and seduces her daughter. I mean, I was just — OK, he didn't look exactly like him, but they were both skinny. And I just went, no, I got my restaurant, I got my kid, for the first time in my whole life I got enough money so I'm not worried about it every waking moment of every single day. I am not tempting fate.

(She is now dressing herself in much more conservative clothing, a long skirt, and a sweater.)

I mean — I'm not saying watching that movie five years ago made me realize I couldn't have a man in my life. It just made me think. So I said NO to Monty and I did without. And you know, it's all right, everybody has to do without something in their lives. A lot of people have to do without the work that they love, I know people, can't get a job, doing the thing that they love, and it's a wound that they carry. You know, really, a great sadness. I think that would be a bigger loss, frankly. 'Cause I have family, my kid is fantastic, and I have friends. My friend Eileen, she doesn't have a boyfriend or a kid, plus for the longest time she was always in and out of work, she's a, one of those, you know — she paints, or photography, or film something — she really is a genius, but she never seems to land somewhere where they'll just let her do what she does, whatever that is at the time. It's hard. And she drinks, you know. Well, why not . . .

(She goes down the hall to Vera's room.)

****

from **The Bells** (2005)
from Act One, Scenes 4, 5, and 6

CHARACTERS

Xuifei

Annette

Mathias

Charlie

Sally

Jim

Baptiste

[*The Bells*, an adaptation of a famous nineteenth-century melodrama, is set in Alaska in 1899 and 1915, approximately the period of the great Alaska Gold Rush. The long-ago murder of the prospector Xuifei comes to light when the French-Canadian Baptiste Carbonneau searches for the answer to the man's disappearance. The lives of the guilt-ridden innkeeper Mathias and his beautiful daughter, Annette, are entwined with Xuifei's disappearance and the Canadian's mysterious arrival.]

SCENE 4

Xuifei.

XUIFEI: There was a girl in my village. When you looked at her, she would return your gaze like a young animal. Her hair fell to her shoulders like water, and although she rarely laughed, her smile was quick. I loved this girl. I wished to marry her. But her family was poor. My love had gone to someone so poor she could never marry and eventually she was sold, by her parents, to a house of prostitution. My brother, knowing my pain, came to me with this news as a gift. See, he said, I will give you money and now you can have her whenever you please. And that is what I did. Night after night I went into the village, and paid for the right to have her. But even that brought me no rest, and I could no longer bear the sight of her face. And so I left my home. I left my home.

(It is night. Mathias is alone in the inn. He has clearly been drinking. Annette enters the scene behind him, as does Xuifei.)

ANNETTE: I can't do it!
XUIFEI: Kuh-yi, kuh-yi.

(Xuifei rubs the balls expertly. She goes to watch him.)

ANNETTE: Show me!

(He does. She laughs, delighted, as he holds her hands and shows her how to rub the balls together.)

XUIFEI: Hao, hun hao!
ANNETTE: Pa, look! I can do it, too!
MATHIAS: Get out of here!

(Xuifei disappears. Annette turns, looks at Mathias, surprised.)

ANNETTE: You all right?
MATHIAS: *(Beat.)* I'm fine, I'm fine. I'm just doing some bills, you got me so worked up about the money this afternoon, thought I'd see what we had in the till.
ANNETTE: You want me to stay with you?
MATHIAS: No, no. You go to sleep.

(She starts to go. He calls to her.)

MATHIAS: *(Continuing.)* Annie?
ANNETTE: Yeah, Pa.
MATHIAS: This Canadian. You like him?

ANNETTE: Oh my God.

MATHIAS: He's educated. Good-looking. French.

ANNETTE: Go to bed, Pa.

MATHIAS: Best-looking guy I've seen around here in years —

ANNETTE: GO TO BED.

MATHIAS: In a minute.

(She goes. Mathias looks at bills that have been left by the cash register, or on the counter.)

MATHIAS: *(Continuing.)* Two, two fifty, four, six — six hundred, just last month — that's down a bit from October, but still enough to put two hundred in the bank, which brings the savings up to over thirty thousand . . .

(After a moment, the sound of the bells, far off, can be heard. He turns, then turns back to his counting. The sound continues to rise as he counts.)

MATHIAS: *(Continuing.)* Thirty thousand dollars, that's nothing to sneeze at, coming from nothing, most everybody else run through it all overnight, but Annette is going to have — her children are going to have more than I ever did. That's what matters. That's what matters!

(He stands, abrupt, listening. The sound fades. He takes another long drink.)

MATHIAS: *(Continuing.)* People showing up out of nowhere, talk about nonsense, it's just the night. Night's so long now. So damn long . . .

(He goes to the counter, turns up the light, which gets brighter and brighter until it suddenly goes out. Blackout.)

SCENE 5

Charlie wandering in the windy night, with Sally and Jim behind him. He is going on. They are drinking and shoving each other, behind him. At some point they simply collapse in a drunken stupor.

CHARLIE: I saw a bird. Last night of my life I slept in a real hotel, this place was swank, people wearing silk clothes, chairs with cushions on 'em. That bird was smart, it could talk in six different languages, some seaman taught him all this shit, then died on him, bird got dumped in this hotel in the wilderness, no one knew much more than that. So I go up to it — and I say, Hey bird! I hear you can talk! What do you have to say for yourself? And the bird just stares at me. So finally I think what the hell, and I turn around, and the bird says, "Thank God he's leaving. Boring old shit head." Turns out he won't talk to nobody unless you're walking away from him. I finally got sick of it, went off and got drunk. Come back, it's three in the morning maybe, I'm climbing the steps to the porch of this place and I hear a woman singing, this song of such purity, it's like a breeze from a far country, moving through the night, a dream of a better time. I never heard anything like it, before or since. And I look through the window, and it's that damn bird. All alone. Singing — well later they told me it was from some opera, that damn bird could sing opera on top of everything else. So the bird finally finishes this — song — and I say to it through the window — Bird, if you can do that — you can sing like that — how come you're so perverse? And that bird looks me in the eye and says, "'Cause you're all sons of bitches."

(He stops, takes a drink. After a moment, Sally laughs, long and hard.)

SALLY: That bird said that?
CHARLIE: *(Laughing.)* It did. "Sons of bitches."
SALLY: That is a smart bird.

(She collapses again. Jim sits up.)

JIM: Where are we?

CHARLIE: We're right about here, you know. There's a windbreak up another half mile, we'll camp there.

JIM: We're sleeping out here? It's cold.

CHARLIE: Dammit Jim, I told you, we're going out to work that old stake Stu Campbell told us on!

JIM: No, come on.

CHARLIE: What'd you think we were doing, you damn drunk?

JIM: You just said . . . I need a drink.

(He staggers over to Charlie, looks for a bottle. Charlie tosses the bottle.)

CHARLIE: We're working now. That stake is still going strong. Stu used to swear on it.

JIM: It's going so good, how come he ain't out there working it?

CHARLIE: What do you care why? Nothing left for any of us in the town.

JIM: Mathias takes care of us.

CHARLIE: I don't want to be taken care of! Goddamn it, I'm not ready to just drink away my last years. I want to do something. I want to feel yearning in my heart. I want to climb into some freezing hell-hole and look for gold. Remember that feeling?

JIM: Yeah, I remember it. That's why I drink, to forget it.

SALLY: *(Sitting up.)* I'm not working any fool ass claim. There's no more gold out there, you fool.

CHARLIE: 'Cording to Stu Campbell there is. He said he and that Chinaman took near six thousand dollars out of the ground up there.

SALLY: That was a long time ago!

JIM: That where we're going?

CHARLIE: I told you this, Jim!

JIM: 'Cause I'm not going there.

SALLY: Jesus God above.

(She looks beyond them. Mathias stands in the snow, covered in blood. They turn and see what she sees. Mathias takes a step forward and tries to speak

to them. After a moment, he collapses. They go to him, pick him up and help him stagger off.)

CHARLIE: Mathias!

SALLY: Oh my God, Mathias! What happened to him?

JIM: Mathias!

CHARLIE: Mathias!

SALLY: Look at all the blood, what happened?

JIM: Can he walk?

CHARLIE: Mathias, can you walk?

SALLY: What's he doing all the way out here? Mathias, what are you doing out here?

CHARLIE: You got him? You got him?

(In dark, Annette rushes through the night.)

ANNETTE: Bring him upstairs, upstairs Mr. Carbonneau! Where did you find him? Oh my God, there's so much blood — somebody make coffee — blankets, I need blankets!

SCENE 6

Baptiste alone in the bar. He peers through the curtain into the back of the house, sees there is no one about, and starts to search the bar area. He pours himself a drink as he searches, then ducks back behind the bar itself, looking. Annette comes out of the house, sees him behind the bar. He does not see her. After a moment, she speaks.

ANNETTE: Can I help you?

(Baptiste stands, startled.)

BAPTISTE: No, no, I . . . ah, no.

(He goes to the other side of the bar. Annette looks back at where he was looking, then looks up at him.)

ANNETTE: Looks like supplies are getting a bit thin back here.

(She pours him a drink.)

BAPTISTE: The prospectors who found your father on the trail, they came here once or twice, you were occupied, caring for him —

ANNETTE: So basically you just let them raid the place for a day and a half.

BAPTISTE: *(A shrug.)* How is he?

ANNETTE: He'll be all right. I guess. I don't know. I haven't thanked you for what you did, Mr. Carbonneau.

(She brings him the drink she poured. He looks at her.)

BAPTISTE: I expected no thanks.

ANNETTE: You carry a man half a mile in the snow, and you don't expect thanks?

BAPTISTE: Expectations are wearisome.

ANNETTE: So are you.

(She turns, upset.)

BAPTISTE: Why are you so angry?

ANNETTE: I'm not angry. I'm grateful. I'm grateful! And I just thought I'd mention that, that I'm grateful that you saved my father's life, 'cause I thought it might be something that was worth saying, thank you, thank you for saving my father's life.

(She pours herself a stiff drink, lifts the glass to toast him.)

ANNETTE: *(Continuing.)* So, thank you!

(He stops her hand. She looks at him.)

BAPTISTE: You're welcome.

(He takes the drink from her and drinks it himself.)

BAPTISTE: *(Continuing.)* You must not drink. It will not help you. *(Beat.)* You are worried for him. Yes? You are worried. For your father.

ANNETTE: I just don't understand what happened. He's been running on about the axe, and it's gone from the woodpile, but I can't make sense of any of it.

BAPTISTE: That is what he used to cut himself?

ANNETTE: It must be, but he says he doesn't remember. I don't know.

BAPTISTE: What was he doing so far out?

ANNETTE: He says he doesn't remember. *(Beat, tearing up.)* I don't know what would happen to me, if anything happened to him. Sorry. I'm just scared. *(Wiping her eyes.)* Do you have family, Mr. Carbonneau?

BAPTISTE: *(Surprised.)* I? What makes you ask?

ANNETTE: I just can't make out why you'd be here. If you did. Why you'd leave them. The world is so lonely, even with there being just one person, that you love. At least my pa and I . . . we have each other.

BAPTISTE: You have your father? And that makes it not lonely?

(She shrugs.)

ANNETTE: No, it's still lonely. I don't know what I mean. It's this place, maybe. I don't know.

BAPTISTE: You think it is not so lonely elsewhere?

ANNETTE: I don't know what it's like, anywhere else, I only ever been here. And everything is so big and . . . distant, here. The mountains and the snow and the black nights can be so black.

BAPTISTE: And you feel alone.

ANNETTE: It is that, but not only that. There's the cold, too, sometimes it's so bitter it reaches right down to the heart of you, and you're thinking you must be a strong person, to bear something so otherworldly, and then the wind comes and you know you can't bear it, you're not strong, you're just like a ghost already, it takes the breath right out of you, just like that. Like death, that's how it feels. So you're going along and feeling that, and wondering how God could make a place so horrible, and you don't know if there is a God, you don't know if there's anything except the cold and the black and the wind, and then the lights come, blue and green and shimmering, all over the night sky. They just come, all at once. You see the stars again. And the mountains are so beautiful, the air is so strong, and you realize this terrible place is where God put his hand, back at the dawn of time. He just reached down and touched the Earth, right here, that's why it's so strong. And then you're not lonely at all. *(Beat.)* But you don't have anyone to tell that to. Which makes it a little lonely, I guess.

(A short beat, then —)

BAPTISTE: My father was a schoolteacher. He was well taught, by the Jesuits; at night he would play badly on the violin, he would quote endlessly from poets whose names are now lost. He was a good man who died needlessly when I was fourteen. My mother married again, a man who drank and beat her children. My sister, one night, he struck her so cruelly. Her face, her body. She was very young. He was a large man, I could not stop him. After her death, I would not stay.

(He pours himself another drink.)

ANNETTE: *(Quiet.)* I'm so sorry.
BAPTISTE: I have seen worse since.

(As he is about to down another drink, she reaches out and places her hand on his, in a small gesture of comfort. He looks up at her, startled. They consider each other. After a moment, Sally and Jim and Charlie enter.)

CHARLIE: How is he?
ANNETTE: He's fine. Just took a couple of nasty cuts, on his arm. That's how come all the blood. He's been unconscious, mostly. I won't say I wasn't real worried there for a minute, but he's come out of it now. *(Then.)* I know you all been helping yourself around here.
SALLY/CHARLIE/JIM: No, no, no —
ANNETTE: No, I was going to say, it's fine. I'm real thankful for your help. Jim Lynch, you take a seat. Sally, let me get you something. What can I get you?

MATHIAS: *(Offstage.)* Annie?

(Annette turns, startled, as Mathias appears in the interior doorway.)

ANNETTE: Pa, what are you doing up? You have to stay in bed.

MATHIAS: I'm all right.

ANNETTE: You're not all right.

MATHIAS: *(Sees Baptiste, bewildered.)* What's he doing here?

ANNETTE: You asked him to stay. He was here, sleeping here, when Sally came and said they found you. On the trail.

SALLY: We found you out on the trail, Mathias, don't you remember? Couldn't carry you back the whole way. So Mr. Carbonneau, he come out and brought you in.

ANNETTE: He saved your life, Pa. Don't you remember any of this?

MATHIAS: Course I do. I'm just tired, is all. Little out of my head, I guess. Sorry.

BAPTISTE: How is your arm?

MATHIAS: Fine. Thanks for your help. Like a drink? Let me get you a drink. Jim, Charlie. She taking care of you? Let me take care of you.

(He goes to the bar, pours drinks.)

ANNETTE: Pa —

MATHIAS: How long I been sleeping?

ANNETTE: A day and a half.

MATHIAS: Guess I was tired. Charlie, Sally — how you holding up for food? You want some eggs, or something?

CHARLIE: I won't say no to a plate of eggs.

MATHIAS: She hasn't fed you yet? Annie, where are your manners?

ANNETTE: I've had a few things on my mind, Pa. And I don't think —

MATHIAS: What?

ANNETTE: I just don't want you to, to, to — Pa, really, you have to —

MATHIAS: I'm all right!

(He hands a glass of wine to Baptiste, pours himself a glass.)

MATHIAS: *(Continuing.)* I'm embarrassed, mostly. Go out to chop some wood for the stove and end up slicing up my own arm, the drunks from the town finding me wandering around the snow like some crazy prospector been lost in the hills since the fever hit.

BAPTISTE: You were a long way out.

MATHIAS: All that white, it's near impossible to find yourself once you're off the landmarks. Wind kicks up, there's no real way of knowing where you are. Isn't that right, Jim?

JIM: That's what I been saying, to Charlie, there ain't none of us in any shape to go out there no more. He's got some crazy idea.

CHARLIE: There's gold out there. Stu Campbell —

MATHIAS: Not tonight, Charlie. Let's just be grateful we're all safe and warm tonight. Annie, what about those eggs?

ANNETTE: *(To Baptiste.)* Don't let him drink too much.

(She takes a moment, then goes. Baptiste watches. Mathias watches him.)

BAPTISTE: *(Off the others.)* She did care for them. While you were sleeping. You've taught her well; she has a generous heart.

MATHIAS: Thank you.

BAPTISTE: Can I ask you about these?

(He holds out the bells. Mathias stares at them for a moment, reaches for them, and takes them from Baptiste, firm.)

MATHIAS: Those things are still lying around, huh? Annie's gonna end up losing them, she's not careful.

(He takes the bells, starts to put them back in their box.)

BAPTISTE: She says it was a Chinaman who gave them to her. A prospector, Stu Campbell, he told me about this Chinaman as well. They worked a stake together, not far from here.

MATHIAS: *(Slight pause.)* You've met Stu Campbell.

BAPTISTE: He said he was a good man. His name was Lin Xuifei. They were friends, it seems, and Campbell thinks something terrible must have happened to him; they had agreed to meet at Minto Landing, and the Chinaman never came.

MATHIAS: And why do you care about that?

BAPTISTE: I was paid to find him.

(A beat.)

MATHIAS: You're a bounty hunter, then.

BAPTISTE: Yes. I am a bounty hunter.

JIM: *(Perplexed.)* Someone put a bounty on the Chinaman? What for? He's been dead —

(Baptiste turns and looks at him. Jim looks at him.)

BAPTISTE: Why do you say that?

JIM: You're the one who said it. You said, Stu thinks something terrible happened to him. I don't know what happened to him.

MATHIAS: I don't know what any of us can tell you. It was a long time ago. None of us knew the man.

BAPTISTE: But he gave your daughter these bells.

(Xuifei appears, holding bells out.)

XUIFEI: Shr-ni-da. Na ba. Na ba.

(Annette enters, takes a step toward him, tentative.)

ANNETTE: What's he saying, Pa?

XUIFEI: Na ba! Na ba!

(Mathias casually takes up the other set of bells.)

MATHIAS: That's right, he came through, he gave those things to Annie, and then he left. Never got them to make that sound again and Lord knows we tried. Charlie, you remember, how long were we trying to get these things to make that sound for her?

CHARLIE: Oh Lord, it was months.

ANNETTE: Show me!

XUIFEI: Hao —

(Xuifei holds her hands and shows her how to make the bells ring.)

MATHIAS: Annie was heartbroken, everybody in town trying to get
these damn bells to sing, nobody can do it. Sally —

SALLY: *(Cool.)* I couldn't do it.

JIM: Just didn't have the touch, not a one of us. She was such a sweet
little thing, you hated to disappoint her.

ANNETTE: You try it, Pa!

(She holds her set of bells out to him. He does not turn.)

MATHIAS: I still can't do it. Here, you give it a try.

*(He hands his set of bells to Baptiste, who looks at them, considers them,
then sets them down.)*

*(Annette turns back to Xuifei, hands him the bells. He shakes his head, and
gives them back to her.)*

XUIFEI: Jeige. Wo geh ni. Wo geh ni.

BAPTISTE: Stu Campbell, this prospector —

MATHIAS: A prospector! You're taking the word of a prospector, each
and every one of them bone mad with gold fever to begin with —
no offense, Charlie —

CHARLIE: None taken —

MATHIAS: By the time they make it through the Chilkoot Pass or what-
not, their brains and their hearts and their souls are frozen solid and
blasted through, not a one of them even resembles a human being by
the time they make it up here, that's who's telling you, what'd he say?

BAPTISTE: He said the Chinaman was carrying three thousand dollars
in gold. Do you remember that?

(Xuifei empties a bag of gold onto his table.)

ANNETTE: Pa, look!

(Xuifei laughs, and gestures her to see it.)

XUIFEI: Ni kan ba. Pyaon lian, shr bu shr?

JIM: That what you're looking for? You talked to Stu, you're thinking
   that Chinaman froze out there, the gold's still out there?

(Xuifei holds a piece up, shows Annette.)

XUIFEI: Wo gei ni.

JIM: That gold is gone!

BAPTISTE: You know that for a fact?

JIM: Everybody knows it! How long ago was that, Sally?

SALLY: Eighteen years.

JIM: That's what I mean!

CHARLIE: There's gold out there still! Stu told me, they never came to
   the bottom of that claim. We're gonna work it, me Sally and Jim.

SALLY: Have a drink, Charlie.

MATHIAS: Gold everywhere. Where is your God in so much gold,
   Carbonneau?

BAPTISTE: My God? I have no relations with God. Do you?

MATHIAS: I fear the Lord. But I question him, too. What I saw those
   years. Men driven mad with the wanting and the having and the losing of it. Standing in the icy waters day in day out, the one becomes
   rich, the next dies of grief and loss, starvation, how many of us, dying
   of cold and starvation, scurvy. You ever see anyone die of scurvy?
   The blood turns thin. Legs go lame. Your gums swell and bleed until
   your teeth drop out, your skin mottles and putrefies — worthy men
   and women turning into lepers around us, my wife, my wife dying an
   unimaginable death, meanwhile God is showering gold without end
   on men living like animals. What kind of God is that?

*(Baptiste does not answer. The two men look at each other, consider each
other. Xuifei stands and slowly leaves the room. Annette takes her bells
and leaves as well.)*

72

MATHIAS: *(Continuing.)* As to this Chinaman and his gold — I couldn't likely say one way or the other, what happened.

BAPTISTE: What year was this? Ninety-nine, ninety-eight?

MATHIAS: Ninety-nine.

BAPTISTE: Was that the year your wife died?

(Mathias looks at him, pours another drink.)

MATHIAS: Yeah, so I had other things to think about.

BAPTISTE: How big was the town at that time, do you remember?

MATHIAS: Lot of people coming through, those years.

BAPTISTE: But those who stayed, those who lived here. How many, thirty, forty?

MATHIAS: That sounds about right.

BAPTISTE: It was a hard winter.

MATHIAS: Yeah, it was.

BAPTISTE: People were starving, you said.

MATHIAS: Yes.

BAPTISTE: How did you make it through?

MATHIAS: You just do! I'm sorry. I don't mean to be so abrupt. It was a hard time. Hard to look back at it. We weren't here long ourselves, just arrived the year before, none of it looking like anything you thought. How could it? People tell you stories of gold without end, they don't tell you the rest, somehow. Met one guy, talked about the Yukon, he called it Eldorado. You hear that, you don't think about ragged men, living in shacks, held against the Northern wind with newspaper and glue. You don't think about the cold, going so deep for so long the memory of warmth moves to a distant place, it becomes the fantasy, a little girl's bedtime story, There once was a place where the sun shone, and things grew. You don't think, how can a woman and a child live in a place like that?

BAPTISTE: Your conscience bothers you, with regard to what you did?

MATHIAS: My conscience?

(A beat.)

BAPTISTE: Bringing them, your wife and child, to this dreadful place.

(A beat.)

MATHIAS: We were poor enough before we came here. I got no way of knowing what my life would've been if we never came. Just as you won't ever know what your life may've been, if you'd lingered on in the elegant city of Montreal, pondering the history of civilization.

(Annette enters, carrying a bowl of eggs and sausages, for Jim and Sally and Charlie.)

ANNETTE: Here you go! It's not much, I did what I could with what was in the kitchen — Pa. What's the matter?
MATHIAS: What?

(Annette sets the food down, worried.)

ANNETTE: Look at you, you're all flushed, you look about to faint —
MATHIAS: I'm fine —
ANNETTE: You're not fine! *(Sharp to Baptiste.)* I told you not to let him drink, it's making him sick. You shouldn't be drinking that stuff, it's been around I don't know how long, it's making you crazy, Pa.
MATHIAS: Guess I'm not used to it.
ANNETTE: Guess not. You're going back to bed right now.

(Annette takes Mathias out. Baptiste turns to the others.)

CHARLIE: I'm sorry we can't help you, son. But no one here really knew that Chinaman. What'd you say his name was?
BAPTISTE: Xuifei. It means "snow."
CHARLIE: Well, that's an interesting fact, but you're missing my point here. We didn't even know his name. We all heard him and Stu were having some good fortune up there on that claim they struck, but he didn't come down here into town but a few times. Kept to himself, mostly. Didn't even speak English. There's not much more to say.

BAPTISTE: There is a good deal more to say, I think. Thank you for your help.

(Baptiste puts his rucksack on his shoulder and goes. There is silence for a moment. Charlie eats.)

SALLY: We got to get out of here.

JIM: That guy's an idiot. He's not gonna find him.

SALLY: He's no idiot.

JIM: You just like him, 'cause he's French.

CHARLIE: What do you want to stick around here for, Jim? I'm telling you, that claim is still out there and that cabin is snug. On top of, Stu left his traps! Catch us a few jackrabbits, steal a couple bottles of hootch from Mathias, we got everything we need.

JIM: *(Abrupt.)* 'Member that Chinaman, how much gold he had? You and me working day and night, we didn't come up with four dollars between us. And he comes in here, a Chinaman, he don't even speak English, and the gold just come out of the earth for him. Rising up, out of the earth, like a bad dream.

(The lights shift.)

****

CHARACTERS

> Clea
> Lewis
> Charlie

[*The Scene* is a dark comedy of manners set in New York City. It opens at a party, where a married, middle-aged, out-of-work actor named Charlie and his friend Lewis talk with a sexy girl named Clea, a newcomer to the big city who has big aspirations. Charlie finds Clea ridiculous at first, but by the second act he has invited her to his home for a sexual romp. The play is both comic and poignant, for Clea will ultimately abandon Charlie, and Charlie will lose his marriage, his friends, and himself.]

> *Charlie, Lewis, and Clea. A corner of a party, loud music, talk, laughter. Charlie and Lewis hold drinks in their hands. Lewis is clearly interested in Clea; Charlie is not.*

CLEA: I love the view here.

LEWIS: *(Surreptitiously checking out her butt.)* Awesome.

CLEA: I mean, mind-blowing, right, it's just so surreal, the lights and the water, it's like unbelievable. I love this loft! Do you know the guy who lives here? He must be incredible. Because I have just no idea, I came with a friend, who knows, like, everybody and I know she told me it was somebody in the fashion industry who I just so had never heard of, my bad. 'Cause he's like, what, like clearly so talented, this place is so beautiful. The water, the air. It's just so surreal.

CHARLIE: How is that surreal?

CLEA: What?

CHARLIE: The air and the water, you said that before, that you found it surreal. How is air and water surreal?

CLEA: Oh you know, it's — just — wow! You know.

CHARLIE: *(To Lewis, annoyed now.)* You want a refill? What is that, a mojito?

LEWIS: Yeah, great.

CHARLIE: How about you, I'm sorry, what's your name again?

CLEA: Clea.

CHARLIE: Would you like a mojita, Clea?

CLEA: No no, I don't drink. My mother was an alcoholic. I mean, she was a wonderful woman and she really loved me but it's like alcohol is so deadly, I mean at these parties sometimes when I'm at a party like this? To stand around and watch everyone turn into zombies around me? It just really triggers me, you know? You go ahead. I mean, that's just for me, I don't impose that on people or anything.

LEWIS: I mean, it's not like, I'm not like a huge drinker, or —

CLEA: Oh good, because you know, I was at this party last week it was such a scene, there were so many people there. You know it was this young director, he's got like seven things going at once, Off Broadway. Can you imagine, the energy level of someone like that? Anyway, it was his birthday party, and they rented out the top two floors of this loft in Chelsea, it was this wild party, like surreal, and then at one point in the evening?

I just realized, that everyone was just totally shit-faced. I mean I don't want to be reactive in situations like that, I don't like to judge people on a really superficial level or anything but it was kind of horrifying. I mean, not that I — you know, drink, you should drink! Enjoy yourselves!

(Lewis and Charlie look at their drinks.)

CHARLIE: Yeah, well, I think I'm gonna head out. Nice to meet you. "Clea."

CLEA: Oh. Whoa. I mean — what does that mean?

CHARLIE: *(Annoyed now.)* What does what mean?

CLEA: "Clea." I mean, "Clea." I mean, whoa —

CHARLIE: Is there a problem?

CLEA: You tell me. You're the one who's all like, "Clea." "Nice to meet you."

CHARLIE: What are you even talking about?

CLEA: Nothing. It just struck me as a little edgy, that's all.

LEWIS: You want me to get those drinks? Why don't I do that? I mean you got to at least talk to Nick, he's gonna show up.

CHARLIE: I'm not talking to Nick. I'm leaving. *(To Clea.)* "Nice to meet you — " is "edgy — "

CLEA: Well, you're totally giving off a vibe here, I'm not making that up. And that is so fine, I mean I do not judge.

LEWIS: Look, Nick's here. Hey Nick —

CHARLIE: I'm not talking to — "A vibe?"

CLEA: Oh is "vibe" like a totally uncool word, in your little tribe —

LEWIS: Hey, Nick!

CHARLIE: No no, it's got a real seventies charm that I find particularly captivating in someone who wasn't born until nineteen eighty-two —

CLEA: Oh, I'm young, well, I guess you're not, huh, that's really the problem isn't it? *(A beat.)*

LEWIS: Whoa.

CHARLIE: There's no problem, Clea. I don't know you. I came by my friend's loft — his name is Edward, by the way, and he's an actor, he's not in "the fashion industry," he's a very fine stage actor even though he's not doing seven Off-Broadway shows at once —

LEWIS: Look, look, look —

CLEA: Yeah, whatever —

CHARLIE: I'm here because my friend asked me to come by, and I did that and now I'm going. Nice to meet you.

CLEA: If there isn't a problem, what are you so bent out of shape about?

CHARLIE: You're really a fucking piece of work.

LEWIS: Charlie.

CHARLIE: What? She's a fucking idiot!

LEWIS: Hey, whoa, are you —

CLEA: No. It's OK. There were, obviously, there were some things said here, that maybe rubbed you the wrong way and I am totally willing to talk about that. I mean I apologize for that. But you were like jumping all over me because I said "surreal," and I just started to feel stupid. So I apologize. If I was edgy or something.

LEWIS: Look, it's OK.

CLEA: Maybe I should get some vodka or something.

CHARLIE: I thought you didn't drink.

CLEA: I don't! I mean, I really don't. Hardly ever.

LEWIS: You want me to get you a vodka?

CLEA: Would you?

LEWIS: Sure.

(He goes. After a minute, Charlie sighs, makes another move to desert her.)

CHARLIE: Listen, I really do have to . . .

CLEA: I totally understand. This is your friend's party, you should go, go, you know a ton of people here probably. You need to talk to Nick, that's clearly a big thing, or something.

CHARLIE: Nick's an asshole.

CLEA: Whatever.

CHARLIE: Look — are you here alone?

CLEA: No! God, no, I came with a friend, I don't know where she is. She's like the total scene-machine.

CHARLIE: Can I ask — I mean — Why do you talk like that?

CLEA: *(Defensive but firm.)* I talk the way I talk. I'm not apologizing for that. I mean, I apologize for before, acting like a little edgy, but language is a totally idiosyncratic and very personal, very organic function of you know, someone's humanity, so I'm not apologizing for my language.

CHARLIE: OK.

CLEA: OK what?

CHARLIE: OK nothing. That's actually a fairly coherent and legitimate point.

****

CHARACTERS

Clea

Charlie

Stella

[Theresa Rebeck uses a traditional theatrical moment — in which a wife walks in on her husband and another woman — to create both comedy and pathos. This scene is both a peak moment in Charlie's relationship with the two women in his life, and the beginning of his downfall.]

Charlie's apartment. Clea and Charlie are having sex on the couch, and elsewhere. They are both in a half state of undress, as if they hit the ground running. It is quite athletic. After an extended and quite vocal climax, they collapse.

CLEA: Oh, God. Don't stop. No, don't stop. Don't stop!

CHARLIE: You got to give me a minute here, Clea.

CLEA: No, don't stop —

CHARLIE: How old did you say you were?

(He means it half as a joke, but it does stop her.)

CLEA: No no don't do that. Don't categorize me.

CHARLIE: *(Still breathless.)* Asking you how old you are is categorizing?

CLEA: You're trying to define age as a life characteristic. As like, something that says something about a person.

CHARLIE: It does say, how old you are.

CLEA: No, it doesn't. It really doesn't. You say, "how old are you" like
I'm young and you're old, like that's some joke, because you think

you're old? But you're timeless. You're like this incredible lion who's
been stalking the Earth since the dawn of nature, or something.

CHARLIE: Tell me, do you actually believe all this crap that you keep
spouting?

CLEA: Of course I believe it. Maybe you should try believing it, too.
Why wouldn't you want to believe that you're a timeless lion? Isn't
that better than thinking you're some old loser who can't get a job?

*(She climbs on him and starts to kiss him. He pushes her away, sudden,
stands and puts his pants on.)*

CLEA: *(Continuing.)* No no. Don't do that. That's what I'm saying, that's
not who you are!

CHARLIE: We have to get you out of here.

(He starts to dress, and straighten out the room again.)

CLEA: We just got here.

CHARLIE: And now we have to go.

CLEA: You said she was going to be at work, all afternoon, she's off
screaming somewhere, come on, you said, we have all afternoon. Be
a lion.

CHARLIE: I think we've had enough of the lion, Clea.

CLEA: I haven't. I mean it. I can go all day, and all night, I could go a
whole weekend. Have you ever done that? Just, spent a whole weekend inside, doing things . . .

CHARLIE: Don't you get sore?

CLEA: You want to find out?

CHARLIE: Jesus! You're like, it's like talking to a porno movie —

CLEA: You are so hung up about the way I talk all the time!

CHARLIE: Well, it's very unusual, Clea, to find someone so remarkably
uninhibited in so many ways —

CLEA: Yeah but you always turn it around, like you don't like it. You
make it sound like it's maybe not so great, the way I am. That I'm
sort of stupid, or just stupid or something —

CHARLIE: *Voracious* is actually the word I was thinking of.

CLEA: Yeah, like that's a bad thing. But you know what? You like it. It's actually driving you crazy how much you like it. Why can't you just say it? If I'm voracious then you're something that wants voracious more than anything it ever saw before.

CHARLIE: How can you know so much and so little at the same time?

CLEA: You have no idea, how much I know. Come on. You said we have all afternoon.

(She kisses him. He is increasingly a lost man. He tries to push her away.)

CHARLIE: We do have all afternoon. Just, not here.

CLEA: Ohhh please . . .

CHARLIE: Listen to me. This is my apartment.

CLEA: I know. I love it that you brought me here. It's so hostile.

CHARLIE: You are really something.

CLEA: Yes, I am. And you're the one who brought me here, to have sex in your apartment.

CHARLIE: Stella could just walk in on us —

CLEA: *(Laughing.)* That would be hilarious.

CHARLIE: Yeah, no, it wouldn't.

(He pushes her away, firm. Looks at her, suddenly simple and clear and a little desperate.)

CHARLIE: *(Continuing.)* I mean, you understand what this is. We're clear on what this is, right?

CLEA: Relax. I know what this is. You're at a place, so am I. This is that place.

CHARLIE: Yes.

CLEA: It's what you need and I want, and that's why it's so hot. Trust me. I understand what this is.

CHARLIE: Good.

(Unsure, hoping that was clear, he leaves the room. She watches him go,

goes to her purse, and takes out an apple, starts to eat, and calls to him in the next room.)

CLEA: *(Yelling.)* You know what we should do tonight? My friend can get me into this party. It's up on the Upper West Side so it is totally not like a really hip scene or anything, but there's going to be some movie stars there, she wouldn't tell me who, but they also have this hot tub there? On the roof. She went to a party at this place a couple weeks ago, and everyone takes their clothes off and gets in the hot tub. And then they have these cater waiters come around, I'm not kidding, with sushi. So you sit in the hot tub and like talk and eat sushi naked. It sounds so nineties, doesn't it? Movie stars and sushi in a hot tub? Maybe they'll play R.E.M. on the "record player." Or do lines of cocaine. It's so unbelievably retro, a hot tub on the roof. I soo want to go.

CHARLIE: *(Entering.)* I've been to this party.

CLEA: Get out.

CHARLIE: I swear to God, I went to that party twenty years ago. Riverside Drive, ninety-six or seven and Riverside.

CLEA: I don't know.

CHARLIE: Sushi and cocaine in the hot tub on the roof? I went to that party. No kidding. I was doing this play Off Broadway, and one of the other actors knew somebody who was going to this party, on the Upper West Side. This rich guy, nobody knew his name, and the place is like a mansion, right, he owns the whole building and it's got Art Deco everything, completely tasteless. The place was huge, like five floors, people screwing in corners of the den and the living room, there was a three-way going on in one room, I'm not kidding, real hedonistic shit. And then there's that hot tub up there on the roof with the greenhouse. *(Laughing now.)* He's got a fucking greenhouse up there, growing cactuses and hibiscus, something, I can't believe I remember this, everybody was completely coked out of their minds, like all night, till five, six in the morning. That's how stupid we all were. It's amazing most of us are still alive. I was such hot shit. That play was unintelligible but I got amazing reviews, and I was . . . the world was on fire for me, boy. Sushi and cocaine and whatever I wanted. God that was fun. That was really fun.

CLEA: Well, guess what, it's your lucky night. Because you can go to that party again. With me.

CHARLIE: *(Reality check.)* I can't go to a party with you.

CLEA: Why not?

CHARLIE: Because I can't.

CLEA: It'll be realllly fun. That's what you said, it was reallly fun.

CHARLIE: I'm not going to a party with you, Clea!

CLEA: No one will see us! That's the whole point, that scene is completely over, so it won't matter!

CHARLIE: Great.

CLEA: You said yourself, the guy who owns this place is so nobody on Earth that is important, just some rich guy with a lot of money and a house with a hot tub, we can totally just go together. I mean, with my friend, we can dump her when we get there, which will be fine with her, she dumps me all the time.

CHARLIE: Look, I have — a life, Clea.

CLEA: Don't you mean, a "wife"?

CHARLIE: Yeah. That's what I mean. And like you said that scene is over. I'm not going to a party with you.

(He continues straightening the apartment.)

CLEA: No, come on, forget about her! You should see how much happier you are when you forget about her. We don't have to go to any party. Let's just pretend we're at a party. We're in the hot tub right now. No. No. Let's skip the hot tub. I like the sound of those rooms, where people are just doing things, in the middle of somebody's house, who they don't even know whose house it is. Let's just think about doing it in front of everybody, in somebody else's room. . . .

(She reaches up and kisses him. He kisses her back. As things are heating

up again, the door opens. Stella enters, and sees them. She stops. After a moment, she speaks.)

STELLA: Charlie. I'm here.

(This is the first Charlie and Clea are aware of her entrance.)

CLEA: Shit.
CHARLIE: Stella.
STELLA: What are you doing, Charlie?
CHARLIE: Nothing. No — this isn't —
STELLA: What, what it looks like? It isn't what it looks like?
CHARLIE: Stella —
STELLA: In my home? You brought, to my home?

(Clea starts to laugh, embarrassed. She tries to stop herself, but simply can't.)

CLEA: I'm sorry. Oh, I am so sorry. But this is just hideous. Oh my God. Wow. It's just so, horrible, and embarrassing.
STELLA: What is she doing here? Don't tell me what she's doing here, I can see what she's doing here. Get out of my house. GET HER OUT OF HERE.
CHARLIE: You have to go.
CLEA: Oh, look. I mean, this is horrible, right, but there's no reason to get all, like, rude. Things have happened here, obviously, but it's not like that's somebody's fault. I mean, I am so not interested in some kind of a ridiculous scene.

(She stands and looks for her clothes.)

STELLA: Oh she's a brain surgeon isn't she? Yeah, this makes complete sense now. I can see why this happened.
CLEA: See this is what I'm talking about! People getting all insulting in a situation like this, why? Is that supposed to help? Because I don't think that is in the least bit helpful.
STELLA: Charlie, get her out of here!

CHARLIE: Clea. Just go.

CLEA: Why should I go? I mean, I was invited here. You and I are doing something here. You made a choice, Charlie, that involved me and not her, and that choice made you happy for the first time in whatever, I mean, you were like fucking miserable until I showed up.

STELLA: Why are you talking?

CLEA: I'm talking because I have something to say!

STELLA: You don't have anything to say! You don't know anything! And you're in my house! This is my house, I pay the rent here, that is my husband, you don't have any rights here!

CLEA: I've been fucking him all afternoon and you haven't. That doesn't exactly give me no rights.

(She sits on the couch, defiant. Stella looks at Charlie, stunned.)

CHARLIE: I'm sorry. Clea. You have to go. We have things, Stella and I have things we need to — this shouldn't have happened, this way, at all, and, and —

CLEA: But it did happen. And you were the one who made it happen. So "should," I think *should* is a very useless word in a situation like this.

STELLA: Charlie?

CHARLIE: I'm sorry. I'm completely in the wrong.

CLEA: Stop. Just stop, already. "In the wrong"?

CHARLIE: *(Furious.)* Clea, do not interfere in this!

CLEA: She's the one who's interfering! Come on, things were fine until she showed up!

CHARLIE: Stop acting like an idiot!

CLEA: You're the one who's being an idiot! "In the wrong"? You're just going to give away your power like that? To her? That's what she wants, that's what she's been about this whole time, "I pay the rent, I want a baby, go suck up to stupid crazy Nick because me and my highlighters rule the world," what about what you want?

STELLA: Is that what you told her? This person, this, you told her —

what did you tell her? Why do I care what you told her, that's clearly the least of, we're married, we've been married for —

CHARLIE: *(Overlap.)* No. No, I did not tell her — this is not, this was not meant to be anything, Stella, this was a mistake —

STELLA: A mistake is forgetting my birthday, Charlie. I don't know what this is. *(She sits, desolate.)*

CLEA: Charlie, are you coming?

CHARLIE: What?

CLEA: Look, we're doing something. Right? We were doing something, before she barged in.

STELLA: I live here! Are you insane? Because you sound insane. You're having an affair with an insane person. Maybe I'm the insane person, I can't, I don't even know, I have, there are — I don't, was your life that bad that you had to let this into it?

CHARLIE: No.

STELLA: Fourteen years, fourteen! You can just, for this? This thing, this isn't a person, even, I don't know what she is —

CLEA: OK —

STELLA: You shut up! You've ruined my life, I don't have to take care of your feelings! Charlie, say something, please! What happened? Why did you do this? Was there some other way I should have been taking care of you?

CLEA: He's a man, he doesn't need a mommy.

STELLA: You know, I will hurt you. I will find some sort of weapon, there's got to be something somewhere, a knife or a vase, anything really is starting to look good, and I will hurt you and we will all end up in the *Daily News*. I promise you, I am not kidding. You need to get out of my house, right now. RIGHT NOW.

CLEA: Look at you, you don't even get it yet! You're just acting like a man, threatening violence and oh you're in charge of everything, why don't you just start waving your highlighters and screaming "Heil Hitler"? If you knew how to keep him, you would've. Look at him! He's just like totally silent around you. He's nobody with you.

Let me tell you something, he isn't like that with me. With me, he's
a lion, roaming the Earth. With me, he's a god!

STELLA: You have got to be fucking kidding me.

CLEA: You don't make him feel the way I do. You don't even begin to
know how. So you can go ahead and hit me, or hurt me, or whatever,
be violent, just like a man? But that's what your problem is. I'm
going, Charlie. You know where to find me.

(She goes. There is a long moment of silence.)

STELLA: Why?

CHARLIE: Don't ask why.

STELLA: *(Suddenly furious.)* Don't ask — why? "Why" is off the table?
You just completely — that was the most humiliating — I'm humil-
iated, Charlie! I'm, I'm everything is, my whole life is suddenly not
even — and for that? And I'm not allowed to ask WHY?

CHARLIE: This is just, I can't — I can't . . .

STELLA: Stop being such a fucking coward and say something!

CHARLIE: You're too competent. *(There is a silence at this.)*

STELLA: What?

CHARLIE: Everything. Gets done. Even when you hate what you're
doing, you get it done. You're like a machine. Everything gets done.

STELLA: *(Almost in tears, suddenly.)* I'm not a machine. That's a lie.

CHARLIE: You're coherent. Everything coheres, and I, I can't — anymore — because I'm — and you're perfect. Your feelings are perfect.
Your work is perfect. You hold down a job you think is stupid and it
frustrates you in the perfect way. Even in how you're not perfect,
even in how things get to you, you're just, even your neurosis is perfect. You're so fucking competent, you don't ever expect too much
out of life. You handle all of it. Even this. Even this! I'm watching
you — you're handling it. You're already going to forgive this.
THAT WAS A FOREGONE CONCLUSION. And then I'll have
that, too. Your competence, and your forgiveness. Oh and your
money, let's not forget that.

STELLA: So this is my fault?

CHARLIE: *(Snarling.)* No! It's my fault! It's my crime! And I own it! It's the only thing you left me, the ability to fuck up, and I want it! It's mine! This fucking disaster is mine, and you can just keep your fucking hands off of it!

STELLA: I don't understand why this is happening. Why are you talking to me like this?

CHARLIE: I'm talking to you like this because this is who I am! And I'm sick of pretending to be perfect, like you, because that is not the person I want to be!

STELLA: This is some sort of fucking midlife crisis. You want to fuck idiotic twenty-somethings because that's what everybody else does, there isn't even a shred of originality in this —

CHARLIE: I wasn't looking for originality, Stella. I was looking to feel like someone who still had a shred of life in him!

STELLA: And fucking great-looking idiots is the only way you can do that? Are you kidding me? I mean it. You don't like your life so you honestly think that screwing that girl — that girl who can hardly speak — who has no character or substance or anything — that that is going to do something, for you, make you whole, make you understand who you are in the world —

CHARLIE: I don't want that. Don't you understand?

STELLA: This is just, it's just self-loathing, Charlie! You're projecting your self-loathing all over the rest of us and destroying everything so you can destroy yourself —

CHARLIE: Thanks, Stell, that's really, this is a thrilling moment to be psychoanalyzed —

STELLA: What else am I supposed to do?

CHARLIE: Nothing! Don't do anything! And don't explain this because I don't want to understand it! I just want to feel something. Remember when you felt things?

STELLA: I feel things!

CHARLIE: You feel unhappy. You feel competent. You feel like a wall.

STELLA: Don't you tell me what I feel. I feel disgust!

CHARLIE: You know what? She's right about one thing. If you want me to stay, you really don't know the first thing about how to make that happen.

(He heads for the door.)

STELLA: Where are you going?

CHARLIE: I'm going to a party.

(He slams the door. Blackout.)

****

THE READING ROOM

YOUNG ACTORS AND THEIR TEACHERS

Harbison, Lawrence, ed. *The Best Women's Stage Monologues of 2007*. Hanover, N.H.: Smith and Kraus, 2007.

Lepidus, D. L., ed. *The Best Women's Stage Monologues of 2006*. Hanover, N.H.: Smith and Kraus, 2006.

SCHOLARS, STUDENTS, PROFESSORS

Brownmiller, Susan. *Against Our Will: Men, Women, and Rape*. New York: Ballantine Books, 1993.

Ellenstein, Peter. In "Theresa Rebeck Gets 'New Voices' Award," *The Buccaneer* (April 3, 2003) www.indy.cc.ks.us/buccaneer/april32003.htm# Theresa%20Rebeck%20Gets%20New%20Voices%20Award

Friedan, Betty. *The Feminine Mystique*. New York: W.W. Norton, 2001.

Greer, Germaine. *The Female Eunuch*. New York: HarperCollins, 2009.

Jenkins, Jeffrey Eric, ed. *The Best Plays Theater Yearbook 2003–2004*. New York: Limelight Editions, 2005.

———. *The Best Plays Theater Yearbook 2006–2007*. New York: Limelight Editions, 2008.

Lark Theatre Company, and Continuing Education Program, The Graduate Center, CUNY. "The Playwright's Role in Fostering Social Change: A Panel Discussion." VHS. Bellingen, New South Wales, Australia: Curio Productions, 2003.

Millett, Kate. *Sexual Politics*. Champaign: University of Illinois Press, 2000.

Morgan, Robin. *Sisterhood Is Global: An Anthology of the International Women's Movement*. New York: The Feminist Press, 1996.

Rebeck, Theresa. *The Butterfly Collection*. Directed by Bartlett Sher. Playwrights Horizons, New York. Penny Ward, video director. VHS. New

---

This extensive bibliography lists books about the playwright according to whom the books might be of interest. If you would like to research further something that interests you in the text, lists of references, sources cited, and editions used in this book are found in this section.

York: New York Public Library for the Performing Arts, Theatre on Film and Tape Archive, 2000.

—————. "Introduction." In *Women Playwrights: The Best Plays of 2001*. Edited by D. L. Lepidus. Hanover, N.H.: Smith and Kraus, 2002.

—————. *Bad Dates*. Directed by John Benjamin Hickey. Playwrights Horizons, New York. Penny Ward, video director. VHS. New York: New York Public Library for the Performing Arts, Theatre on Film and Tape Archive, 2003.

—————. *Mauritius*. Directed by Doug Hughes. Manhattan Theatre Club and Huntington Theatre Company. Parker/Hodges Productions. VHS. New York: New York Public Library for the Performing Arts, Theatre on Film and Tape Archive, 2007.

—————. *Our House*. Directed by Michael Mayer. Playwrights Horizons, New York. Penny Ward, video director. DVD. New York: New York Public Library for the Performing Arts, Theatre on Film and Tape Archive, 2009.

Rebeck, Theresa, John D. Brancato, and Michael Ferris, *Catwoman*. DVD. Directed by Pitof. Burbank, Calif.: Warner Home Video, 2005.

Schlafly, Phyllis. *Feminist Fantasies*. Dallas: Spence Publishing Co., 2003.

Theater Talk "Tony Shalhoub, Theresa Rebeck, and Gutenberg! The Musical." Directed by Adam Walker. VHS. New York: Theater Talk Productions, 2007.

—————. "Mauritius, and Charles Busch on Die Mommie Die!" Directed by Adam Walker. VHS. New York: Theater Talk Productions, 2008.

Third Watch: The Complete First Season. DVD. Burbank, Calif.: John Wells Productions, Warner Home Video, 2008.

THEATERS, PRODUCERS

Chinoy, Helen Krich, and Linda Walsh Jenkins. *Women in American Theatre*. New York: Theatre Communications Group, 2006.

Jenkins, Jeffrey Eric. *The Best Plays* series. Pompton Plains, N.J.: Limelight Editions.

ACTORS, DIRECTORS, THEATER PROFESSIONALS

Bermel, Albert. *Farce: a History from Aristophanes to Woody Allen*. Carbondale: Southern Illinois University Press, 1990.

Esslin, Martin. *The Theatre of the Absurd*. Garden City, N.Y.: Anchor Books, Doubleday, 1969.

Goodman, Lizbeth, with Jane de Gay, ed. *The Routledge Reader in Gender and Performance*. London: Routledge, 1998.

Hays, Michael, and Anastasia Nikolopoulu, ed. *Melodrama: The Cultural Experience of a Genre*. New York: St. Martin's Press, 1999.

THE EDITIONS OF THERESA REBECK'S PLAYS USED FOR THIS BOOK

Rebeck, Theresa. *Collected Plays Volume I, 1989–1998*. Hanover, N.H.: Smith and Kraus, 1999.

—————. "No Exit." In *HB Playwrights Short Play Festival 2003: The Subway Plays*. William Carden and Pamela Berlin, eds. Hanover, N.H.: Smith and Kraus, 2004.

—————. *Complete Plays Volume II, 1999–2007*. Hanover, N.H.: Smith and Kraus, 2007.

—————. *Complete Plays Volume III, Short Plays 1989–2005*. Hanover, N.H.: Smith and Kraus, 2007.

—————. *Mauritius*. New York: Samuel French, 2008.

Rebeck, Theresa, and Alexandra Gersten-Vassilaros. *Omnium Gatherum*. New York: Samuel French, 2003.

SOURCES CITED IN THIS BOOK

Antonio, Mervin P. "Interview with Theresa Rebeck," Program, Humana Festival, March 2007.

Backalenick, Irene. "On the Aisle," *Westport (CT) News* (November 25–December 2, 1998).

Bernardo, Melissa Rose. "Three Girls and Their Brother," *Entertainment Weekly* (March 28, 2008).

Bilowit, Ira J. "Looking Good in 'Spike Heels,'" *Backstage* (May 29, 1992).

Blake, Leslie (Hoban). "Rebeck on a Roll," *Encore* (September 1996).

Brantley, Ben. "Kate Burton, Carrying a Load of Grief in 'The Water's Edge,'" *New York Times* (June 15, 2006). http://theater.nytimes.com/2006/06/15/theater/reviews/15edge.html.

—————. "Three Thugs and a Stamp Collection," *New York Times* (October 5, 2007). http://theater.nytimes.com/2007/10/05/theater/reviews/05maur.html.

Broadway.com Staff. "Did Theresa Rebeck's New Play Push Critics to the Edge?" *Broadway.com* (June 15, 2006). www.broadway.com/buzz/did-theresa-rebecks-new-play-push-critics-to-the-edge/.

Burney, Christopher. Introduction to *Theresa Rebeck Complete Plays Volume III*. Hanover, N.H.: Smith and Kraus, 2007.

Canning, Charlotte. *Feminist Theaters in the U.S.A.* New York: Routledge, 1996.

Engelman, Liz. *The Bells Resource Guide*. Princeton, N.J.: McCarter Theater Center, 2005. www.mccarter.org/Education/The-Bells/15.html.

Feingold, Michael. "Uncollected Stories," *The Village Voice* (October 10, 2000).

——————. "Mauritius," *The Village Voice* (October 17–23, 2007).

Greene, Alexis. "Family of Mann," *TheaterWeek* (July 18–24, 1994).

——————. "View of the Dome," *TheaterWeek* (October 14–20, 1996).

——————. "Theresa Rebeck." In *Women Who Write Plays: Interviews with American Dramatists*. Hanover, N.H.: Smith and Kraus, 2001.

Gutman, Les. "The Water's Edge," *CurtainUp* (June 15, 2006). www.curtainup.com/watersedge.html.

Huff, Richard. "'Brooklyn Bridge'? I Was Shoved," *New York Daily News* (June 26, 1994): 3.

Hughes, Douglas. Interview about Theresa Rebeck with Alexis Greene. December 27, 2009.

Hurwitt, Robert. "Risk, Repartee Deliver Exhilarating 'Mauritius,'" *San Francisco Chronicle* (June 3, 2009).

Isherwood, Charles, "All About Ego, Showbiz and a Little Black Dress," *New York Times* (January 12, 2007). http://theater.nytimes.com/2007/01/12/theater/reviews/12scen.html.

——————. "When a Star Takes a Turn Awaiting a Star Turn," *New York Times* (November 8, 2009). http://theater.nytimes.com/2009/11/06/theater/reviews/06understudy.html.

Jacobs, Leonard. "Mauritius," *Backstage* (October 4, 2007). www.backstage.com.

Jones, Chris. "2003–2004 Best Play: Omnium Gatherum," in *The Best Plays Theater Yearbook 2003–2004*. Edited by Jeffrey Eric Jenkins. Pompton Plains, N.J.: Limelight Editions, 2005.

Kiesewetter, John. "Kenwood Native Delves into Criminal Mind on 'Law & Order,'" *The Enquirer* (November 18, 2001). www.enquirer.com/editions/2001/1/18/temkenwood_native.html.

Klein, Alvin. " 'Spike Heels' Ponders Women's Dilemmas," *New York Times* (November 14, 1993): Sunday edition, Connecticut sec., pp. 18, 19.

——. "If Oprah Went to Nora's House," *New York Times* (March 11, 2001): 13.

Kuchwara, Michael. "'Omnium Gatherum' Features Dinner, Debate," AP (September 25, 2003).

Lahr, John. "Pay and Play," *The New Yorker* (October 15, 2007): 102.

McKinley, Jesse. "Please Pass the Salt (and the Terrorism)," *New York Times* (September 21, 2003): sec. 2, p. 5.

McNulty, Charles. "Review: 'Mauritius' at Pasadena Playhouse,'" *Los Angeles Times* (April 7, 2009). http://latimesblogs.latimes.com/culture monster/2009/04/reviewmauritius-at-pasadena-playhouse.html

Minkoff, Michelle. "Theresa Rebeck's Labor of Love Returns to Where It Began," *College Media Network* (December 6, 2005). https://media .www.thejusticeonline.com/media/storage/paper573/new/2005/12/06 /Arts/Theresa.Rebecks.Labor.Of.Love.Returns.To.Where.It.Began-1122142.shtml

Minor, E. Kyle. "Theresa Rebeck Does It Her Way," *Westport (CT) Minuteman* (April 28, 1994): B18.

Moore, John. "'Our House': A Hammer to TV, Media," *Denver Post* (January 17, 2008). www.denverpost.com/theater/ci_7991563.

Morphos, Evangeline. "Theresa Rebeck by Evangeline Morphos," *BOMB* magazine (Fall 2006). www.bombsite.com/issues/97/articles/2858.

Murray, Matthew. "Mauritius," *Talkin' Broadway* (October 4, 2007). www .talkinbroadway.com/world/Mauritius.html.

Orel, Gwen. "The Water's Edge," *Backstage* (June 14, 2006).

Raidy, William A. "Shrew Does the Taming in 'Spike,'" *Newark Star-Ledger* (June 5, 1992).

Rebeck, Theresa. "Cracking Broadway," *New York Times* (June 13, 1999): Sunday edition, sec. 2, p. 4.

——. *Free Fire Zone: A Playwright's Adventures on the Creative Battlefields of Film, TV, and Theater.* Hanover, N.H.: Smith and Kraus, 2006.

——. *The Understudy.* (Unpublished manuscript.)

——. www.theresarebeck.com.

Rebeck Clippings. Billy Rose Theatre Division, New York Public Library for the Performing Arts.

Rich, Frank. "Reversing the Stereotypes in the War of the Sexes," *New York Times* (June 5, 1992): C3.

———. "Omnium Gatherum," *New York Times* (October 5, 2003): sec. 2, p. 1.

Richards, David. "The Hollywood Sitcom World and the Egos Behind the Scenes," *New York Times* (June 29, 1994).

Rizzo, Frank. "Mauritius," *Variety* (October 30, 2006): 59.

Siegel, Naomi. "THEATER REVIEW: Melodrama in the Land of the Noonday Moon," *New York Times* (April 3, 2005). http://query.nytimes.com/gst/fullpage.html.

Simonson, Robert. "The Butterfly Collection," *Time Out* (October 5, 2000): 159.

———. "An Acute Interest in Bad Behavior," *New York Times* (September 23, 2007). www.nytimes.com/2007/09/23simo.html.

Sommer, Elyse. "Mauritius," *CurtainUp* (October 5, 2007). www.curtainup.com/mauritius.html.

Sommers, Michael. *Newark Star-Ledger* (September 26, 2003).

Tallmer, Jerry. "La-La Land in New York: Theresa Rebeck's 'The Family of Mann,'" *Backstage* (June 24–30, 1994): 15.

Taylor, Markland. "Abstract Expression," *Variety* (December 7, 1998).

———. "Dollhouse," *Variety* (March 26, 2001): 56.

Teachout, Terry. "Scenes From the Farcical Stage of Life," *Wall Street Journal* (November 6, 2009).

Verini, Bob. " 'Mauritius' at Pasadena Playhouse," *Variety* (April 6, 2009).

Weber, Bruce. "THEATER REVIEW: Like Father (a Writer), Like Son (an Actor), and Neither Is Likable," *New York Times* (October 4, 2000).

White, Diane. "Forced Through Celebrity's Many Circles of Hell," *Boston Globe* (March 9, 2008).

Awards

"And the winner is . . . "

THEATER

IRNE (Independent Reviewers of New England) Award for Best New
   Play, *Mauritius,* 2007
Elliot Norton Award, *Mauritius,* 2007
Pulitzer Prize Finalist, *Omnium Gatherum,* 2003
Otis Guernsey New Voices Award, *The Bells,* 2003
Barrie and Bernice Stavis Playwriting Award, National Theatre
   Conference, 1994

TELEVISION

For *NYPD Blue*
The Edgar Award, Mystery Writers of America
Writers Guild of America Award for Best Writing for a Drama Series,
   Episodic
The Imagen Award, honoring positive portrayals of Latinos and Latino
   culture in entertainment
The Peabody Award, recognizing the most outstanding achievements
   in electronic media

	PULITZER PRIZE	TONY AWARD	NY DRAMA CRITICS CIRCLE AWARD		
			Best American	Best Foreign	Best Play
1988	Alfred Uhry *Driving Miss Daisy*	David Henry Hwang *M. Butterfly*	No Award	Athol Fugard *Road to Mecca*	August Wilson *Joe Turner's Come and Gone*
1989	Wendy Wasserstein *The Heidi Chronicles*	Wendy Wasserstein *The Heidi Chronicles*	No Award	Brian Friel *Aristocrats*	Wendy Wasserstein *The Heidi Chronicles*
1990	August Wilson *The Piano Lesson*	Frank Galati *The Grapes of Wrath*	No Award	Peter Nichols *Privates on Parade*	August Wilson *The Piano Lesson*

This awards chart is provided for reference so you can see who was winning the major writing awards during the
writing career of the playwright.

	PULITZER PRIZE	TONY AWARD	NY DRAMA CRITICS CIRCLE AWARD		
			Best American	Best Foreign	Best Play
1991	Neil Simon *Lost in Yonkers*	Neil Simon *Lost in Yonkers*	No Award	Timberlake Wertenbaker *Our Country's Good*	John Guare *Six Degrees of Separation*
1992	Robert Schenkkan *The Kentucky Cycle*	Brian Friel *Dancing at Lughnasa*	August Wilson *Two Trains Running*	No Award	Brian Friel *Dancing at Lughnasa*
1993	Tony Kushner *Angels in America: Millennium Approaches*	Tony Kushner *Angels in America: Millennium Approaches*	No Award	Frank McGuinness *Someone Who'll Watch Over Me*	Tony Kushner *Angels in America: Millennium Approaches*
1994	Edward Albee *Three Tall Women*	Tony Kushner *Angels in America: Perestroika*	Edward Albee *Three Tall Women*		
1995	Horton Foote *The Young Man From Atlanta*	Terrence McNally *Love! Valour! Compassion!*	Terrence McNally *Love! Valour! Compassion!*	No Award	Tom Stoppard *Arcadia*
1996	Jonathan Larson *Rent*	Terrence McNally *Master Class*	No Award	Brian Friel *Molly Sweeney*	August Wilson *Seven Guitars*
1997	No Award	Alfred Uhry *The Last Night of Ballyhoo*	No Award	David Hare *Skylight*	Paula Vogel *How I Learned to Drive*
1998	Paula Vogel *How I Learned to Drive*	Yasmina Reza *Art*	Tina Howe *Pride's Crossing*	No Award	Yasmina Reza *Art*
1999	Margaret Edson *Wit*	Warren Leight *Side Man*	No Award	Patrick Marber *Closer*	Margaret Edson *Wit*
2000	Donald Margulies *Dinner with Friends*	Michael Frayn *Copenhagen*	No Award	Michael Frayn *Copenhagen*	August Wilson *Jitney*
2001	David Auburn *Proof*	David Auburn *Proof*	David Auburn *Proof*	No Award	Tom Stoppard *The Invention of Love*
2002	Suzan-Lori Parks *Topdog/Underdog*	Edward Albee *The Goat: or, Who Is Sylvia?*	Edward Albee *The Goat: or, Who Is Sylvia?*		
2003	Nilo Cruz *Anna in the Tropics*	Richard Greenburg *Take Me Out*	No Award	Alan Bennett *Talking Heads*	Richard Greenburg *Take Me Out*

	PULITZER PRIZE	TONY AWARD	NY DRAMA CRITICS CIRCLE AWARD		
			Best American	Best Foreign	Best Play
2004	Doug Wright *I Am My Own Wife*	Doug Wright *I Am My Own Wife*	Lynn Nottage *Intimate Apparel*		
2005	John Patrick Shanley *Doubt, a Parable*	John Patrick Shanley *Doubt, a Parable*	No Award	Martin McDonagh *The Pillowman*	John Patrick Shanley *Doubt, a Parable*
2006	No Award	Alan Bennet *The History Boys*	Alan Bennett *The History Boys*		
2007	David Lindsay-Abaire *Rabbit Hole*	Tom Stoppard *The Coast of Utopia*	August Wilson *Radio Gulf*	No Award	Tom Stoppard *The Coast of Utopia*
2008	Tracy Letts *August: Osage County*	Tracy Letts *August: Osage County*	Tracy Letts *August: Osage County*		

INDEX

The entries in the index include highlights from the main In an Hour essay portion of the book.

100

ABOUT THE AUTHOR

Alexis Greene is an author, editor, and teacher specializing in theater and women's studies. Greene has written or edited nine books about theater, most recently *Front Lines: Political Plays by American Women*, an anthology of contemporary dramas that she edited with the playwright Shirley Lauro (The New Press). Other books by Greene include *The Lion King: Pride Rock on Broadway* (Hyperion), with Julie Taymor; *Women Who Write Plays* (Smith and Kraus); *Lucille Lortel: The Queen of Off Broadway* (Limelight Editions); *Women Writing Plays* (University of Texas Press); and *The Story of 42nd Street* (Random House), written with Mary C. Henderson. She edited the art catalogue that accompanied the 2008–2009 exhibition *Curtain Call: Celebrating a Century of Women Designing for Live Performance*, organized by the New York Public Library and the League of Professional Theatre Women. Greene holds a Ph.D. in Theater from the CUNY Graduate Center and has taught at Vassar College, Hunter College, and New York University. She was cofounder and first president of Literary Managers and Dramaturgs of the Americas, is on the board of the League of Professional Theatre Women, and is a member of New York Women's Agenda, PEN, and The Authors Guild. She lives in New York City with her husband, Gordon R. Hough.

ACKNOWLEDGMENTS

The author particularly wishes to thank Theresa Rebeck, not only for her remarkable plays but also for being a dedicated participant in their ongoing digital conversation. The author extends her thanks to In an Hour's extraordinarily patient editor, Susan C. Moore, and to Marisa Smith and the Smith and Kraus publishing team for this invaluable series.

NOTE FROM THE PUBLISHER

We thank Theresa Rebeck, whose enlightened permissions policy reflects an understanding that copyright law is intended to both protect the rights of creators of intellectual property as well as to encourage its use for the public good.

Know the playwright, love the play.

Open a new door to theater study, performance, and audience satisfaction with these Playwrights In an Hour titles.

ANCIENT GREEK

Aeschylus   Aristophanes   Euripides   Sophocles

RENAISSANCE

William Shakespeare

MODERN

Anton Chekhov   Noël Coward   Lorraine Hansberry
Henrik Ibsen   Arthur Miller   Molière   Eugene O'Neill
Arthur Schnitzler   George Bernard Shaw   August Strindberg
Frank Wedekind   Oscar Wilde   Thornton Wilder
Tennessee Williams

CONTEMPORARY

Edward Albee   Alan Ayckbourn   Samuel Beckett
Theresa Rebeck   Sarah Ruhl   Sam Shepard   Tom Stoppard
August Wilson

To purchase or for more information
visit our web site inanhourbooks.com